From SUZUKI *to* MOZART

A History of the Repertoire in Suzuki Violin Books 1-10

Hadley Johnson

ISBN: 1479105317
ISBN-13: 9781479105311
Library of Congress Control Number: 2012914886
CreateSpace Independent Publishing Platform
North Charleston, South Carolina

*This book is dedicated to the other
two sides of my Suzuki Triangle:
my mother, Susan Johnson, and
my first teacher, Kathleen Spring.*

TABLE OF CONTENTS

DISCLAIMER:

This work represents the view of its author, and does not necessarily represent the view of the International Suzuki Association or its regional associations. These materials are not intended to replace authorized Suzuki® Method teacher training or study with a qualified Suzuki teacher.

INTRODUCTION:
THE "SUZUKI" METHOD

In the final stages of writing this book I interviewed William Starr, a teacher who went to Masumoto, Japan to observe Shinichi Suzuki and became one of his good personal friends. After explaining some of the motivation behind Dr. Suzuki's Book 1 compositions, he told me that Dr. Suzuki never wanted this method to be named after himself. Rather, he preferred the name "the mother tongue method applied to the violin." The birth of the method occurred when Suzuki had the insight that all knowledge can be acquired in the same way that Japanese children learn to speak Japanese. He started experimenting with the idea that any ability, even one as difficult as playing a stringed instrument, can be fostered by creating a nurturing environment similar to that in which children learn their native language.

I grew up with the Suzuki method, starting my violin lessons at age eight with Kathleen Spring. At that time, twenty-seven years ago, the method was fairly new in my hometown. I don't recall having any intense desire to play the violin, but in my family music was required and the piano teacher wouldn't take me until I turned ten. Dr. Suzuki, writing about his method in *Nurtured by Love*, described a situation that sounds very similar to my early years with the violin:

> It was a result of circumstances that [she] played the violin. Whether [she] liked it or disliked it is not the question. Precisely as all Japanese children learn the Japanese language, and learn it by heart, to like or dislike it had no bearing at all. It was exactly the same.

Mrs. Spring was a great teacher. She loved children and knew how to bring out the best in us. I know that I will appreciate her contributions to my upbringing my entire life. My mother showed up to every lesson faithfully. The entire family was very supportive of everything I did with the violin. Gradually, over the course of time, I began to really enjoy my instrument. Because of all of my early training I was able to get into the St. Olaf Orchestra under the direction of Steven Amundson, another great teacher who truly changed my life for the better.

As I grew older, I began to think of the Suzuki method as childish and, frankly, a bad way to train a young violinist. Too much listening, too little creativity. Prodigy building without knowledge. These were some of the thoughts that I had in my early twenties. Somehow I had forgotten the philosophy behind the Suzuki method.

Once again, purely by accident, I was reintroduced to the Suzuki method. My mother talked me into taking a teacher training course, to which I reluctantly agreed. The training changed my life again. Mrs. Spring, who was also my teacher trainer, finally brought home to me that the Suzuki method is a means of building character. It is not just about the violin; the violin is merely a vehicle for leading a good life. Aren't we all searching for the best kind of life? Isn't that what we want for our children? To have happy, contented lives?

Every criticism I've heard about the Suzuki method, and I've heard plenty, indicates a lack of something. "Suzuki kids don't learn to read music." "Suzuki students don't learn to think for themselves." "Suzuki students don't learn about rhythm." The list goes on and on.

The Suzuki method is not a means of withholding knowledge from children; it is just a different way of acquiring it. We would never accuse a child of lacking in verbal creativity as an adult because his first word is "mama," just the same as everyone else's first word is "mama." We would never ask an infant to start writing before speaking, just as we would never ask a two-year-old to read the newspaper as soon as she could put together a full sentence. A child is not expected to move out and get an apartment as soon as he can walk.

No, there is an order and a pace to childhood learning, and if we try to start very young children on instruments, we have to respect that the process will take time. A great number of repetitions are required before anything is learned, but when it is learned it becomes so ingrained that it appears instinctual. Young children still depend very much on their parents, and they will have an easier time learning if the parents are involved. The entire family has to participate to create success. Children learn through play, so Suzuki made everything that he taught accessible through games. One of his chief attributes was his sense of humor when working with children. Every skill associated with music; reading, theory and history; will develop if it is a part of the child's upbringing. The Suzuki Method can incorporate every facet of musical knowledge if done properly.

Dr. Suzuki's method led to incredible results. He never required an entrance exam, but all of the students who followed his direction progressed and became good musicians. Tiny children performed complex classical works. Many of his students went on to become extremely successful as adults. Toshia Eto became a professor at Curtis Institute. Koji Toyoda became the concertmaster of the Berlin Radio Symphony Orchestra.

People flocked to Masumoto from all over the world to learn his secret. Some thought that the magic was the order in which he taught pieces, leading to an almost fanatical adherence to the method books. (Incidentally, at the beginning Suzuki was changing the order of the books with such regularity that his publisher finally put his foot down and told him to stabilize it. This led to the order as it is today.) It is important to realize that it is not the pieces in the books, or memorizing everything, or any of these little details of the Suzuki myth that lead to success. Success lies in Suzuki's philosophy that all children have the ability to learn, and that we, the teachers and parents, have the responsibility to create an environment in which that learning is nurtured. As Suzuki would say, "never hurry, never rest." With enough repetitions, ability of any kind can and will be developed.

HOW TO USE THIS BOOK

This book is designed to be an easy music history reference for parents and teachers of the violin school of the Suzuki Method. It may also be used by students, though its format may not be very approachable for younger children.

The pieces are listed in the same order as they are found in the Suzuki books. An alphabetical list of composers and pieces is at the end of the book. There is a chapter dedicated to each Suzuki book. The background of composers, individual pieces and, in some cases, genre information is included. These genres include the Baroque dance suite, the sonata, and the concerto, which are explained in detail in the basics section at the beginning of the book. If you have any ideas, corrections or more information about the music, I welcome feedback! My email address is: hadleyejohnson@gmail.com.

In my studio we have used this information for recital programs or narrations (students are welcome to copy entries from this book verbatim for performances). In some cases I have found chamber music that corresponds to the particular level and style of pieces in the books. At the end of the book are some examples of music history games that teachers can play with their students.

A NOTE ABOUT TITLES AND NOTATIONS

One of the initial challenges when writing this book was figuring out how, exactly, titles of the pieces and musical terms should be written. Was I supposed to italicize? Underline? Which letters should be capitalized? Ultimately I used *Writing about Music: A Style Sheet,* by D. Kern Holoman. *The Chicago Manual of Style* uses this book as its reference. I used *The Chicago Manual of Style* as well as Holoman's book to format my footnotes and works cited.

STARTING WITH THE BASICS: THE ERAS OF MUSIC

THE BAROQUE (1590-1750):

The word "baroque" means "misshapen pearl." It was originally a pejorative term used by conservatives to describe the gaudiness of a new era, gaudiness which began with architecture and visual art and extended into music. This contrasted with the clarity, simplicity, and symmetry of earlier Renaissance ideas.[1] An alternate translation of baroque is "bizarre," if we are going to refer to its original meaning.[2] In the later twentieth century historians started to call music written between 1590 and 1750 a part of the Baroque tradition, and the compositions that remain are well loved.[3]

Some historical events of note during the Baroque era were the Thirty Years War (a devastating conflict between Catholics and Protestants that destabilized much of Europe), several outbreaks of the plague and the colonization of the Americas.[4] It was an era during which superstitions about witchcraft and sorcery were prevalent (thousands of people were burned), and scientists first began to understand that the Earth was not the center of the universe.[5] Intellectuals of the seventeenth century philosophized about political equality and capitalism, generating ideals which would be put into practice in future centuries.[6]

The Baroque era was a time of tremendous innovation in composition. For example: the symphony, opera, the concerto and the solo sonata did not exist before the seventeenth century.[7] Unexpected dissonance played a much greater role, as might be expected in music that had as its primary goal moving the emotions of the listener.[8] Many of these new ideas came from Italian composers, and when their music became popular throughout Europe other composers responded by creating their own styles (most notably French and German).[9]

The goal when playing Baroque music is to have a "crisp, clear manner of articulation, as opposed to sluggish treatment."[10] Often music was not written as it was meant to be played: for example, slow movements were supposed to be improvised with trills and mordents

---

1   Garretson 36
2   Pauly 2
3   Burkholder 288
4   Garretson 38-9
5   Garretson 39
6   Burkholder 287
7   Burkholder 287
8   Burkholder 288
9   Burkholder 288
10   Garretson 51

that were not indicated in the music. Dotted notes were lengthened and the complementary notes shortened, a process called "double-dotting."[11] Tempos were moderate,[12] retard and accelerando did not exist,[13] and dynamics are commonly thought to have been terraced because crescendo and diminuendo were impossible on keyboard instruments.[14] (Terraced dynamics are a sudden change from loud to soft, which creates an echo effect.) There is some debate about the use of crescendo and diminuendo with other instruments, as the violin and certainly the voice were capable of gradations in volume.

Instruments built between 1590 and 1750 looked and sounded different than the instruments of today. The violin was shorter and the bow shaped very differently. The lack of a screw on the bow made changing its tension impossible. Because of these dissimilarities a Baroque violin is softer in volume than the modern instrument.

Much of the Baroque music we have today was "rediscovered" in the Romantic era by composers such as Mendelssohn and Brahms. Because it is through the filter of Romanticism that all Baroque music comes to us, many musicians choose to avoid strict period interpretations in favor of more dramatic performances. Another argument for romanticizing Baroque music is that it is almost impossible to achieve pure Baroque style with a modern instrument.

Composers of the Baroque era include Lully, Bach, Fiocco, Handel, Veracini and Vivaldi.

CLASSICAL (~1750-1820)

The word "classical" has many different meanings. It can, for example, describe art that has stood the test of time[15] or anything that

---

11 Garretson 50
12 Garretson 58
13 Garretson 65
14 Garretson 66
15 It is a relatively new practice to have a set of standard repertoire that is played over and over again in concert halls. Composers who wrote before the nineteenth century were forced to write what seem to be almost impossible quantities of music. Many of them had to write new sonatas or symphonies every week or risk losing their jobs. Today this sort of prolific composition is considered evidence of genius; in their day it was merely a part of being a professional musician.

pertains to ancient civilizations.[16] In this book Classical refers to a period of time between the Baroque and Romantic eras, roughly extend-
ing between 1750 and 1820. (One way to avoid confusion is to note
that the Classical era is capitalized and other connotations of classical
are in lower case.)

The Classical period is conventionally divided into several categories. The top four are: *galant, empfindsamer stil* (sensitive style),
Enlightenment and *Sturm und Drang* (storm and stress).[17] *Galant* style
was elegant and refined, still ornate but less grand than Baroque music.[18] It was "modern, chic, smooth, easy and sophisticated,"[19] unlike
the strict contrapuntal compositions that came before. (*Galant* style,
like early Baroque music, can be considered a response to the prevail-
ing trend.) The *empfindsamer stil* was written with an eye to the middle class, its definition of sensitivity "attitudes of honesty and good-
ness . . . often approach[ing] the borders of sentimentality."[20] (In Jane
Austen's novel *Sense and Sensibility* the word "sensibility" has the
same essential meaning as *empfindsam*: the capacity for being affected
emotionally or intellectually.[21]) The Enlightenment philosophies of ra-
tionalism and optimism were also expressed through music written
during this period. *Sturm und Drang* was a reaction against the other
three styles, in particular in its search for emotional truth and the importance of the imagination.[22] It is by far the most dramatic form of
Classical music. Though these forms seem very different, they can all
be lumped under the category "Classical" as much for their universal
appeal as for the dates they were written.[23] Simplicity, balance and
order make these pieces enjoyable for most audiences.[24]

Classical society was, in general, more polite than Baroque. The
aristocracy patronized beauty and elegance in art.[25] Moderation carried

16   Pauly 3
17   Garretson 81
18   Garretson 82
19   Burkholder 480
20   Garretson 82
21   Webster's New World Dictionary *Sensibility*
22   Garretson 82-3.
23   Pauly 4
24   Pauly 4
25   Garretson 84

the day when it came to music. Crescendo and decrescendo weren't as extreme as they would be during the Romantic era.[26] Tempo was usually somewhere around an average pulse rate, that is, between 60 and 80 mm.[27] The texture of music was less complex than that of the Baroque, favoring lightness and simplicity.[28] Vibrato and tone color were becoming more important, and should be added in moderation when a student is preparing pieces written during the Classical era.[29]

Mozart, Rameau and Gossec were all Classical composers.

ROMANTIC

The Romantic period coincides with the Industrial Revolution and drastic changes of class structure in Europe.[30] I do not include dates, because there are several different schools of thought determining when the Romantic period began and ended. The simplest is to call all music composed between 1800 and 1900 Romantic. The Romantic era is sometimes considered coterminous with what historians call the "long nineteenth century" which began with the French Revolution in 1789 and ended with World War I in 1914. Finally (bizarrely), the Romantic period can be said to have begun in 1803 with Ludwig van Beethoven's growing deafness and his resulting change in compositional style. [31]

Because of the technological advances of the Industrial Revolution, composers had more instruments at their disposal and many of the preexisting instruments had been modified for a wider range of pitch and dynamics. A growing middle class produced greater numbers of amateurs with the free time to practice, amateurs who were able to play more sophisticated music than in previous eras. Most musicians no longer had to rely on aristocratic patrons, as this middle class was able to support public concerts. Orchestration in music, for example, the symphonies of Mendelssohn, Berlioz and Beethoven, called for more instruments.[32]

---

26   Garretson 92
27   Garretson 90
28   Garretson 94
29   Garretson 94
30   Garretson 103
31   Burkholder 576
32   Garretson 104

Many of the changes in composition occurred as a result of the influence of Ludwig van Beethoven, a man whose first works continued in the Classical tradition and who eventually became a major catalyst for Romantic-style innovations. He was financially independent for a great deal of his life, allowed by a stipend to spend as much time as he wanted on a single work. Unlike composers before him, for example Wolfgang Amadeus Mozart, who were required to churn out immense quantities of music or starve, he could strive for perfection in each of his publications without financial ruin. For this reason Beethoven was able to survive on nine symphonies rather than the hundreds required of Classical composers. Many of Beethoven's most stirringly emotional works were written after (and perhaps because of) the onset of deafness. These later compositions inspired the next generation of musicians to venture out of the polite confines of Classical style and into a new era.

Though Romantic style is for the most part distinguished by its sheer diversity, there are some common threads. There was, for example, a greater emphasis on the individual as a musician. Composers were considered interesting if they had their own style, even more so if they had fascinating life histories.[33] Romantic music had a greater intensity of feeling, for example optimism or morbidity, than music of the past.[34] The idea of escapism, particularly the escape back to an idyllic, and perhaps imaginary, pre-industrial past was popular.[35] Some composers, such as Dvořák, began to display nationalism in their works by incorporating folk music.

Thomas, Schumann, Brahms and Paganini are examples of romantic composers.

THE BAROQUE DANCE SUITE

The Suzuki books are filled with movements from Baroque dance suites. During the Baroque era, the word "suite" was interchangeable with "set," "partita," "sonata," and "lesson."[36] In general the Baroque

33 Longyear 9
34 Longyear 10
35 Longyear 11
36 Fuller 665-6

dance suite followed this progression: prelude, allemande, corrente, sarabande, optional dances (including the minuet, bourrée and gavotte) and gigue.[37] This order was not necessarily set in stone. Often composers added an extra dance or left one out.

It is easier to understand the order of the Baroque suite if its practical function is explained: The dance suite was originally written for community get-togethers that lasted several hours. In order for the participants to avoid tiring too quickly, the dances varied from fast to slow. Alternations in speed allowed the dancers a period of rest between fast numbers.[38] Alan Pedigo describes a possible scenario:

> The orchestra might begin a dance series with a fanfare in order to claim attention. This would lead immediately into an intrada, which is slow enough to limber properly, even for the oldest leg muscles and effect unison of the assemblage. After an instant of pause, the music would call for a dance rhythm of greater energy, such as a gavotte. A brief pause would then introduce a sarabande, which would decelerate, but maintain, the momentum of the occasion so that the dancers could regain their breath and allow their tired muscles to relax. Now the rejuvenated dancers are ready to dance an allemande, branle or corrente with jubilation. Another recuperation is achieved while slowing to the pace of a siciliano or ritornello. The dance ends in a blaze of glory with the intensity demanded by a giga or tarantella.[39]

At times the movements of suites were carefully constructed to go together as a whole, but more often they were initially each meant to stand alone and eventually thrown together as a publication gimmick.[40] Movements within a given suite are usually different in character, though there may be subtle variations on the same harmonic material.[41] (One example of this kind of variation is Bach's Partita No. 2 for solo violin, which is based on the chorale "Krist lag in Todesbanden.")

---

37 Winold 8
38 Pedigo 2
39 Pedigo 2
40 Fuller 666
41 Winold 8

There seemed to be very little about the dance suite that was ever completely standardized. Yet one thing in particular is always common to the movements of a suite: the key is the same throughout.[42] Probably this aspect has more to do with the limitations of Baroque instruments than anything else: a set of sheet music would be purchased for a group of musicians, some of whose instruments would only be able to play in one key.

Suggested speeds for the different dances are as follows:

Preludio = 50-60 to the quarter note
Sarabande = 45-65 to the quarter note
Allemande = 100-180 to the quarter note
Corrente = 180-220 to the eighth note
Gavotte = 120-180 to the quarter note
Giga = 140-180 to the dotted quarter note

The origin of the Baroque dance suite is murky. Renaissance dance sets seemed to have no particular order. By the late Renaissance and early Baroque, sets were paired into fast and slow dances as explained previously. By the early seventeenth century, however, the allemande, courante, and sarabande had become standard.[43] The first gigue published at the end of a dance suite was written by Johann Jacob Froberger in 1649.[44]

By 1750 the dance suite had become old-fashioned. For the most part it had ceased to be background music for dances and had turned into something merely to play and listen to. Because composers had originally lengthened the suites with numerous da capos and repeats – to turn short pieces of music into full dances – they considered it practical now to shorten the pieces.[45] This new form became the Baroque sonata.[46] Composers started focusing elsewhere, continuing to develop

---

42   Fuller 667
43   Winold 8
44   Winold 9
45   Some of the minuets and gavottes in the Suzuki books are interminable. In my opinion, unless the student is actually planning on accompanying Baroque dancers, some of the repeats and da capos can be eliminated.
46   Pedigo 4

genres such as the concerto and the symphony.[47] The binary form of a typical Baroque dance provided the template for the sonata-allegro form, which is the backbone of Classical symphonies, concertos and chamber works. The suite in its Baroque form would appear later as a vehicle for nineteenth and twentieth century composers who looked to the past for inspiration. One example is Edvard Grieg's famous "From Holberg's Time, Suite in the Old Style," written in 1884 and played by public high school orchestras ever since.

THE BAROQUE CONCERTO

Following is a brief introduction to the Baroque concerto and its antecedents, too brief to go into much detail. A more comprehensive explanation can be found in Arthur Hutchings' book *The Baroque Concerto*. (The concertos within Suzuki Books 1-8 are all Baroque concertos. Mozart's concertos in Books 9 and 10, written during the Classical era, are almost a different genre. They do, however, derive from these earlier works.)

The very first works named "concerto" were in fact for choir with instruments. The Renaissance "canzona" was more like our modern conception of the concerto, that is, a piece for stringed instruments with continuo.[48] The word "concerto" seemed to have a variety of different connotations before it settled on its current usage. It was generally used in the same way as the word "consort," that is, the singing or playing together of two or more people, and was synonymous with the word "sonata."[49] All three (sonata, concerto, and consort) came from the madrigal, which could be either sung or played.[50] Because it was originally a vocal term, it

> reflected a former devotion to singing, for the sonatas and con-
> certos played by the Vitalis, Torelli, Valentini, Corelli, Vivaldi,
> Geminiani, Veracini and others upon Amati's and Stradavari's

---

47   Winold 9
48   Hutchings 19
49   Straeten 47
50   Straeten 47

instruments mark a golden age of the string ensemble that is comparable with the previous golden age of vocal ensemble.[51]

The violin became one of the top choices for early concerto composers because it was considered a substitute for the human voice, a substitute which had the same expressivity without limitations of range or fatigue.[52]

Trio sonatas were probably the earliest Baroque forebears of the concerto.[53] These sonatas originated from the dance suite, and often had corresponding movement names such as "gavotte" or "minuet." When these sonatas began to be used for worship services, tempo markings rather than dance names were deemed more appropriate. For performance purposes, an "allegro" was simply a "gigue" with church clothes on. Trio sonatas typically had two upper stringed instruments (violins) and two continuo instruments (harpsichords and viola da gambas were considered "continuo" instruments and served in an accompanying capacity). Two continuo instruments were needed because instruments of that time were much quieter than their modern counterparts. Trio sonatas when played with modern instruments only really require one continuo part. They make ideal chamber music for intermediate string players (starting in Books 5 or 6), especially for those who have the common difficulty of coming up with a violist.

The concerto grosso, a genre made popular by Archangelo Corelli in the 17th century (see Courante from Book 7), was an expansion of the trio sonata.[54] A small ensemble of stringed instruments would play the ripieno parts (similar to tutti), and the *concertino* parts were played by two solo violins and a cello.[55] Concertino players joined the rest of the orchestra when not employed with their solos. The designation

---

51   Hutchings 23
52   Hutchings 23
53   Hutchings 19
54   There is some controversy whether or not it was Arcangelo Corelli or Giuseppe Torelli who first invented the concerto grosso. Torelli was the "first to write sonatas in several parts with one or more obbligato instruments to which he gave the name of Concerti" (Straeten 136). Torelli's Concerti Grossi Op. 8 was published posthumously, and could have predated Corelli's (Straeten 136).
55   White 3

concerto grosso was intended to inform the producer that a larger number of musicians was required rather than the smaller string quartet, or *concerto a quattro*.[56]

The concerto reached a new level when it was tackled by the Venetian school of composers in the early 1700s, a group which included Antonio Vivaldi. These were the first composers to standardize the three-movement form: fast – slow – fast. Another convention, inspired by Venetian opera, is the use of ritornello in the first and third movements and aria-like second movements.[57] (Ritornello is a recurring tutti section, deriving from instrumental interludes between stanzas in opera.[58]) Bach's Concerto in A Minor uses these same forms. He was directly influenced by Vivaldi's work, having at one time transcribed some of the Venetian master's multi-violin concertos for harpsichord.

In many ways these early concertos were the same as concerti grossi, with one notable exception: the level of difficulty. Chapell White writes that they "were very close relatives, indistinguishable in structure and similar in style and purpose. . . Even in the early stages, however, virtuosity was a stronger element in the solo concerto than in the concerto grosso."[59] The solo Baroque concerto, then, is the next step for the student who has entered Suzuki Book 4.

There is some confusion about the plural of the word "concerto." Should it be "concertos" or "concerti"? *The Harvard Dictionary of Music* and *Writing about Music: A Style Sheet* by D. Kern Holoman (authoritative enough to be used by *The Chicago Manual of Style*) uses the Anglicized plural "concertos." The word "concerti" is, however, correct if the concertos are listed in a title that is entirely in Italian or if it is a part of the plural of concerto grosso: concerti grossi.[60]

---

56   Hutchings 22
57   Hutchings 135
58   Randel 733
59   White 4
60   The same is true of another problem word, "cellos." In general when writing about music in the United States all foreign spellings of words (even British English) are seen as affectations and should be avoided.

THE BAROQUE SONATA

Use of the term "sonata" was at first merely a designation that a piece of music was written for an instrument other than voice.[61] Over the course of its evolution, a piece called a "sonata" could also have been named a "canzona" around 1650, "sinfonia" and "concerto" around 1700, and "lesson" and "solo" in England in the 18th century.[62]

One of the only real constants in the sonata was the slow-fast-slow-fast succession of movements and the tendency to stay in one key[63] as is found in the dance suite. By the second half of the seventeenth century a distinction was made between varying types of sonatas: the church sonata (*sonata da chiesa*) and the chamber sonata (*sonata da camera*).[64] The two can generally be distinguished by the names of the movements: church sonatas had abstract names that reflected the mood of the piece, for example "largo" or "allegro," and chamber sonatas had dance names such as "allemande" or "giga". Eventually the church sonatas started to be called "sonatas" and the chamber sonatas "partitas" or "suites."[65]

Within the wide parameters of slow-fast-slow-fast, sonatas tended to be fantasies. A fantasy is essentially whatever the composer felt like writing at the time rather than a set form.[66] In 1701 the French music theorist Sebastian de Brossard described the fantasy element of the sonata as

> . . . varied by all sorts of emotions and styles, by rare or unusual chords, by simple or double Fugues, etc., etc., all purely according to the fantasy of the Composer, who, being restricted by none but the general rules of Counterpoint, not by any fixed meter or particular rhythmic pattern, devotes his efforts to the inspiration of his talent, changes the rhythm and the scale as he sees fit, etc."[67]

---

61   Newman "The Sonata in the Baroque Era" 6
62   Newman "The Sonata in the Baroque Era" 20-1
63   Staying in the same key was especially prevalent in the *sonata de camera*.
64   Straeten 136
65   Newman "The Sonata in the Baroque Era" 21
66   Newman "The Sonata in the Baroque Era" 24
67   Newman "The Sonata in the Baroque Era" 24

The violin continued evolving in the eighteenth century into its modern form and as a result playing techniques changed, increasing the possibilities of range and dynamics.[68] During this time the violin sonata was also in transition. Now that the violin was capable of more, passagework became increasingly varied.[69] The third movement of the sonata rather than the first was closest to the modern concept of sonata form.[70] (See below for a definition of sonata form.)

By the end of the Baroque era, the mid eighteenth century, sonata composition had diverged into two camps: the followers of Corelli, who sought beauty of form and style, and the violinists who "cultivated the virtuoso element to gain the admiration of the multitude by dazzling them with their fireworks."[71] Veracini's compositions seem to fall in the second category.

As time went on, the term "sonata" was used for almost every form of instrumental music. William Newman, the writer of several authoritative books on the sonata published in the latter half of the twentieth century, has listed the traits that seem to hold true for almost all sonatas written during the Baroque era. Sonatas, Newman says, are instrumental pieces usually written for one to four players. They have contrasting movements (slow-fast-slow-fast). They are "absolute" rather than "programmatic" music—they never have a "plot." And finally, sonatas usually lack utilitarian purposes such as providing music at a dance.[72]

The term "sonata" is related but not identical to the term "sonata form." A sonata was simply an instrumental piece as described above. Sonata form is a blueprint for composing a movement of a piece of music: exposition followed by development and ending with recapitulation. In the exposition the composer presents a theme and establishes a tonic key. This tonic then modulates into the dominant.[73]Often the exposition is repeated and ends with a strong cadence (that is, it sounds as if the piece could be over when the exposition finishes). In the development, the original theme can be fragmented or keys changed rap-

---

68   Straeten 180
69   Straeten 180
70   Since then it has become standard for the first movement to follow sonata form.
71   Straeten 180
72   Newman 7
73   Rosen 1

idly or reworked. At times a new theme is introduced. The development ends with a transition back to the original key and theme.[74] This is the recapitulation, which restates the exposition, this time ending in the tonic key rather than the dominant. Sometimes the recapitulation is followed by a coda.[75] Use of sonata form was very popular during the late eighteenth century, when many Suzuki works were written.

Charles Rosen notes that using this specific template to define sonata form for the 18th century is not entirely accurate, because the form evolved through time and was essentially different for each composer. It was only after the form had been in use for at least a hundred years that anyone bothered to define it. These definitions are found in the following works on composition: in 1826 the *Traité de haute composition musicale* vol. II by Antonin Reicha (close personal friend of Ludwig Beethoven), in 1845 *Die Lehre von der musikalischen Komposition* vol. III by Adolph Bernhard Marx (great admirer and promoter of Beethoven) and in 1848 *School of Practical Composition* by Carl Czerny (pupil of Beethoven).[76] Thus our outline for sonata form is at best a generalization of Baroque or Classical trends (if that) and a model for works written in the latter part of the nineteenth century. [77] Not surprisingly, Ludwig van Beethoven's works are often used to define sonata form.

---

74   Rosen 2
75   Rosen 2
76   Rosen 3.
77   Rosen 3

CHAPTER 1: SUZUKI BOOK 1

FOLK SONGS

Book 1 starts with several folk songs. By their very nature, folk songs change with time, language, new words and different regions of the world. Any true folk song's origins are unknown.

It is entirely possible that the Suzuki versions of these tunes are different from the ones that you learned growing up. According to good folk song tradition, tunes have been changed to suit current needs: in this case, for pedagogical purposes or to make them fit the limitations of a beginning instrumentalist. Many of these folk tunes are of German origin, probably familiar to Dr. Suzuki because of his time spent studying in Berlin.

TWINKLE, TWINKLE LITTLE STAR

The earliest record of the tune for *Twinkle, Twinkle Little Star* was found in a Mr. Bourin's (first name unknown) *Les Amusements d'une Heure et Demy* (the amusements of an hour and a half) in 1761.[78] It seems to originally have been a French folk tune known as *Ah! Vous Dirai-Je, Maman* (Ah! I tell you, Mama!).[79] Little else is known about the origin of the melody. The tune showed up in various guises, most

---

78   Fuld 593

79   Fuld 593. The words to "*Ah, Vous dirai-je Maman!*" are not entirely appropriate for younger readers, so I will omit them from this text.

famously as the inspiration for the variations by Mozart (1778).[80] It was eventually used as the melody for a number of English poems such as *Baa Baa Black Sheep*, *ABC*, and *Twinkle Twinkle Little Star*.

The words for *Twinkle, Twinkle Little Star* were written in a poem by Jane Taylor under the name "The Star" and published in 1806 (more than forty years after the tune had first been written down!).[81] It only works with the tune if the first two lines of each verse are repeated at the end of the verse. The first verse seems to work as a song, but the other verses don't make much sense when put together with the tune.

Twinkle, twinkle, little star,
How I wonder what you are,
Up above the world so high,
Like a diamond in the sky.

When the blazing sun is set,
And the grass with dew is wet,
Then you show your little light,
Twinkle, twinkle, all the night.

Then the traveler in the dark,
Thanks you for your tiny spark,
He could not see where to go
If you did not twinkle so.

In the dark blue sky you keep,
And often through my curtains peep,
For you never shut your eye
Till the sun is in the sky.

As your bright and tiny spark
Lights the traveler in the dark,
Though I know not what you are,
Twinkle, twinkle little star.[82]

---

80   Fuld 593
81   Fuld 594
82   George, ed. 184

VARIATIONS ON TWINKLE

The Twinkle Variations were written by Dr. Suzuki with the purpose of teaching short Baroque bowstrokes. (Note that the first variation has the same rhythm as the beginning of the Bach Concerto for Two Violins!) They are easy for children to control and can be gradually lengthened. Six variations of Twinkle also give the student a great deal of time to really let good pre-twinkle habits set in!

LIGHTLY ROW

Lightly Row was originally a hunting song, written around 1710 according to the *Erk-Böhme Deutscher Liederhort* (a book of folk songs collected by Ludwig Erk in 1892).[83] The tune fits at least two sets of German words. The first is *Alles neu macht der Mai* (May makes everything new), which has as its first verse:

Alles neu macht der Mai, macht die Seele Frisch und frei.
Lasst das Haus! Kommt hinaus! Windet einen Strauss!
Rings erglänzet Sonnenschein, duftend pranget Flur und Hain;
Vogelsang, Hörnerklang tönt den Wald entlang.

(May makes everything new, makes the soul fresh and free.
Leave the house! Come outside! Make a bouquet!
The sun is shining everywhere, field and grove are smelling fresh;
The woods are full of birdsong and the sound of the horn.)

These words were written by H. von Kampen in 1818.[84] The other version familiar to German children is *Hänschen klein* (little Hans):

Hänschen klein ging allein in die weite Welt hinein;
Stock und Hut steht ihm gut, ist ganz wohlgemut.
Aber Mutter weinet sehr, hat ja nun kein Hänschen mehr;
"Wünsch dir Glück," sagt ihr Blick, "kehr nur bald zurück!"[85]

---

83   Kneip 418-19
84   Kneip 311
85   Kneip 311

(Little Hans went alone into the great wide world;
He looks good with his stick and cap, he is feeling well.
But his mother is crying, because she doesn't have little Hans anymore;
"Good luck," say her eyes, "but come back soon!")

The entire song tell the story of little Hans, who, after seven years out in the world, grows up and comes back to the great rejoicing of his mother and sister.

SONG OF THE WIND

Song of the Wind seems to have its origin in Germany, where the melody was first known to have been set to the words *Gänsedieb* (goose thief). In 1824 Ernst Anschutz fit the melody to a similar story: *Fuchs, du hast die Gans gestohlen* (fox, you stole the goose). [86] Following are the German words and a translation:

Fuchs, du hast die Gans gestohlen
Gib sie wieder her,
Gib sie wieder her,
Sonst wird dich der Jäger holen mit dem Schiessgewehr,
Sonst wird dich der Jäger holen mit dem Schiessgewehr.

Fox, you've stolen the goose,
Oh, give it back!
Oh, give it back!
Or surely the hunter will get you with his shotgun,
Or surely the hunter will get you with his shotgun.[87]

GO TELL AUNT RHODY

Go Tell Aunt Rhody is a folk song of New England. It was possibly begun as a play-party song, which was simply a song with clapped accompaniment. The name "Rhody" can authentically be substituted for

---

86 Pinkert-Sältzer 302
87 Pinkert-Sältzer 289

the name of any aunt you prefer.[88] The traditional words (following the theme of goose mortality begun in "Song of the Wind" and admittedly a little depressing) are as follows:

1. Go tell Aunt Rhody, go tell Aunt Rhody, go tell Aunt Rhody the old gray goose is dead.
2. The one she's been saving (3 times) to make a feather bed.
3. She died in the mill pond (3 times) standing on her head.
4. She died on a Friday (3 times) with an aching in her head.
5. The old gander's weeping (3 times) because his wife is dead.
6. The goslings are crying (3 times) because their mama's dead.[89]

Many violin teachers make up their own lyrics to the folk songs, and this piece in particular could use some heavy editing in order to be less frightening to the pre-k set. The other danger of learning the original words is that it tends to make the student add notes that are not in the book.

O COME LITTLE CHILDREN

This song is not technically a folk song, as its origins are known. Johann Arbaham Peter Schulz wrote the melody in 1794, and in 1811 the priest Christoph Schmidt turned it into a Christmas carol.[90] Schmidt at the time was already well known as the writer of *Bible Stories for Children*. Following are his lyrics, now popularly used for *O Come Little Children*:

Ihr Kinderlein, kommet, o kommet doch all!
Zur Krippe herkommet in Bethlehems Stall
Und sieht, was in dieser hochheiligen Nacht
Der Vater im Himmel für Freude uns macht.

O come, little children, o come one and all!
O come to the cradle in Bethlehem's stall!

---

88 Krull 42
89 Krull 42
90 Pinkert-Sältzer 304

And see what the Father, from high heav'n above
Has sent us tonight as a proof of His love.[91]

MAY SONG

The earliest known version of *May Song* is *Nun so reis ich weg von hier* (Now I am traveling away from here), which was written down around 1690.[92] The German poet H. Hoffmann von Fallersleben (1798-1874) later wrote the words that are in more common usage in Germany today:

Alle Vögel sind schon da, alle Vögel, alle!
Welch ein Singen, Musiziern, Pfeifen, Zwitschern, Tireliern!
Früling will nun einmarschieren, kommt mit Sang und Schale.

All the birds are already here, all the birds, all!
What singing, music making, whistling, tweeting and chirping!
Spring is coming now, coming with song and sounds.

THOMAS HAYNES BAYLY
1797- 22 April 1839
Long, Long Ago
Era: Romantic, published 1843
Genre: Song

Thomas Haynes Bayly was an English songwriter and dramatist. He intended to go into the church as a profession but his marriage to a wealthy woman ended his studies early.[93] Six years later one of his sons died, he lost his health, and he was running out of money. Bayly started writing in order to make a living.[94]

Long, Long Ago was the most popular song in the United States in 1843, shortly after it was published in a Philadelphia magazine. Bayly

---

91 Pinkert-Sältzer 177
92 Kneip 312
93 Nelson-Burns http://www.contemplator.com/england/longago.html
94 Nelson-Burns http://www.contemplator.com/england/longago.html

titled the song *The Long Ago*, but his editor Rufus Griswold probably changed it to its current name: *Long, Long Ago*.[95] Bayly himself never enjoyed the popularity of *Long, Long Ago*, as the song was published four years after his early death at age 42. Following are the original words:

Tell me the tales that to me were so dear,
Long, long ago, long, long ago.
Sing me the songs I delighted to hear,
Long, long ago long ago.
Now you are come all my grief is removed.
Let me forget that so long you have roved.
Let me believe that you love as you loved,
Long, long ago, long ago.

Do you remember the path where we met,
Long, long ago, long, long ago,
Ah, yes, you told me you ne'er would forget,
Long, long ago, long ago.
Then, to all others my smile you preferred,
Love, when you spoke, gave a charm to each word,
Still my heart treasures the praises I heard,
Long, long ago, long ago.

Tho' by your kindness my fond hopes were raised,
Long, long ago, long, long ago,
You by more eloquent lips have been praised,
Long, long ago, long ago.
But, by long absence your truth has been tried,
Still to your accents I listen with pride,
Blessed as I was when I sat by your side,
Long, long ago, long ago.[96]

The melody in the Suzuki books is identical to the original melody, making it possible to teach kids the real words without the inevitable pitfall of playing the wrong notes or bowings.

---

95   Nelson-Burns http://www.contemplator.com/england/longago.html
96   Agay 78-9

SHINICHI SUZUKI
17 October 1898 – 26 January 1998
Allegro, Perpetual Motion,
Allegretto (*Muss i denn*), Andantino, Etude

> The real essence of art turned out to be not something high up
> and far off. It was right inside my ordinary daily self. The very
> way one greets people and expresses oneself is art. If a musician
> wants to become a fine artist, he must first become a fine person.
> – Nurtured by Love[97]

Following is a synopsis of the book *Nurtured by Love*, written by
Shinichi Suzuki. It is a combination of his autobiography and a history of his teaching method, which he termed "talent education." All
teachers who use the Suzuki books should read *Nurtured by Love* in
its entirety, however, and not rely on this short description of his life
and work.

Shinichi Suzuki was born in Nagoya, Japan, to a family that owned
a violin factory. He was the oldest child. As a boy he was brought up
to expect that he would work in the family business of making instruments, and his primary use for violins was as weapons in playful fights
with his siblings.

When he was a teenager and just about ready to graduate from
commercial school, his family acquired a gramophone and he had his
first real experience with the emotional pull of violin music in Mischa
Elman's rendering of *Ave Maria*. As a result Suzuki picked up one of
the violins from the factory and tried to learn how to play it himself.
He eventually turned the entire focus of his young life to learning to
play the violin, starting with teachers in Japan and eventually studying
for eight years in Berlin, Germany. While there he met and married his
wife, Waltraud.

Suzuki was very much influenced by the writings of Leo Tolstoy
and the words of his father, constantly seeking the best way to live
his life. One of his beliefs was that it was important to seek out great
men and learn from them. For example, while in Berlin he befriended
Albert Einstein and joined him in many musical evenings (Einstein

---

97   Suzuki 83

played the violin very well). Suzuki's primary teacher in Berlin was Karl Klingler, a man that he admired as much for his humanity as for his skill at the violin. Through the music of Mozart, Suzuki came to see art as a means to achieve a higher understanding of the human soul. He believed that the sadness of our births and eventual deaths is overcome if everything in our lives is directed toward loving each other. Much of his philosophy on life and art was built during his formative years and would become an important part of his teaching method.

Suzuki returned to Japan when his mother became ill, with the plan that he and his wife would eventually move to Switzerland. Instead he became a professor of violin at a university. One day he was asked to teach a four-year-old boy named Toshiya Eto. All his life Suzuki had been an object of fascination to children, often followed around by them like the pied piper. Nonetheless he was reluctant to teach the boy, and he asked the child's father to wait while he thought about how he would teach him. In the middle of a quartet rehearsal that week he was suddenly struck by the idea that all Japanese children speak Japanese. If they could learn such a difficult skill at such an early age merely by being surrounded by it, what would stop a child from learning an instrument in the same way? He decided to teach the boy, starting with creating an environment at home that surrounded him with violin music. He believed that *kan*, knowledge that seems instinctual, is actually bred in children through constant repetition. The little boy learned to play the violin at a prodigious rate, stunning everyone who heard him.

World War II interrupted Suzuki's professorial career. He spent the end of the war building floats for seaplanes in a small village up in the mountains. While there he experienced the extremes of hunger and desperation, and the only comfort he had to give his factory workers was to play his violin. After the war Suzuki decided that he no longer wanted to do repair work on older students. Instead, he wanted to develop a system of infant development. What happened then was the birth of the Talent Education program at Masumoto, a place where he could put to work all of the ideas that he had for teaching small children.

The success stories of Suzuki's students has become almost legendary in violin circles. Children of six years were playing Vivaldi and Bach concertos, and as adults they were also phenomenal successes. Toshiya Eto went on to become a professor at Curtis Institute. One of them became the concertmaster of the Berlin Radio Symphony Orchestra. Teachers flocked from all over the world to watch Dr. Suzuki teach.

Suzuki seemed to be more saddened than pleased by his reputation as a prodigy builder. His lifelong goal was to build character through ability and to allow adults to keep some of the joy and love they so often lose after childhood. He considered one of his greatest successes as a violin teacher to be a student who became a mayor of a town and was reelected again and again because his constituents loved him so much.

According to William Starr, a man who went to Masumoto and became a close personal friend of Dr. Suzuki, these pieces have the following pedagogical purpose:

Allegro's first four notes are from a Japanese folk tune. Dr. Suzuki used these four notes to work on a fast bow stroke, increasing the length of the bows with time and repetitions. One of his students asked him to make the exercise more interesting, leading Suzuki to change it to the piece as it is today.

Perpetual Motion was meant to work on lots of separate bow strokes without too many complicated string crossings. The many possible variations of Perpetual Motion make it ideal for the instruction of many other skills as well. (For example, it can be the student's first piece that is centered on the D string.)

Allegretto is derived from the German folk song *Muss i den.* It is in the key of D, continuing the work of becoming comfortable on the D string started in Perpetual Motion. The jumping notes are a preparation for arpeggios.

Andantino is scalar in character. It is much easier to learn than Allegretto, giving the students some time to really master playing on the D string.

Etude is characterized by many string crossings and a departure from the relatively simple forms of previous pieces. In particular the first two notes (raising both arms to the D-string level from A and back) are difficult for students to accomplish. Many people thought that Etude was too complex for children to memorize, but because

Dr. Suzuki wanted it in the books it was added anyway. (The idea that Suzuki's success was based on the exact order of the pieces in the books led at times to unquestioning obedience to his sequence.) Though it is fair to say that this piece is extraordinarily complicated and perhaps confusing to students, the extra weeks it takes to memorize it and keep track of which melody goes where gives the student even more time to make a habit of good string crossings.

JOHANN SEBASTIAN BACH, CHRISTIAN PEZOLD AND ANONYMOUS
Bach: 21 March 1685 – 28 July 1750
Minuets 1, 2 and 3
Era: Baroque, written around 1717
Genre: Baroque dance suite

Johann Sebastian Bach was born in Eisenach, Germany, and was the youngest of eight siblings in a very musical family. The Bachs had been so influential in the musical life of Eisenach that for years after the last Bach had left town musicians there were known as *die Baache*[98] (Bachs).

Bach's first instrument was the violin, and his father was his first teacher.[99] At nine years old he was orphaned and moved in with his older brother in Ohrdurf. His brother was a professional organist and

---

98 David 21
99 Seaton 310

probably introduced him to keyboard instruments. Bach continued his studies and lived with his brother until he turned fifteen, when he was encouraged to set out on his own.[100]

From 1700 through 1717 Bach moved to a series of different towns, at first continuing his studies and then taking jobs as an organist or cantor. He lived in Luneburg, Weimar, Arnstadt, Mulhausen, and Weimar again (where he played the violin as concertmaster).[101] He wrote music that was consistently too difficult for the musicians with whom he worked and then had no patience for their "incompetence."[102] Bach regularly offended his employers with his superior attitude, at times even leading to disciplinary action. His job from 1717-1723 at Anhalt-Cothen was probably his favorite term of employment, working for a prince who was both very interested in music and a skilled musician himself.[103]

Bach's next job was working as Kantor and music director of the Thomasschule in Leipzig. He was considered a mediocre choice for the job, but got the position as the other two preferred candidates went elsewhere.[104] Though he never quite saw eye-to-eye with the musical authorities in Leipzig, and was at one time labeled "incorrigible" for his frequent unannounced trips out of town and neglect of his singing master duties, he stayed there for the rest of his days.[105] Bach was famous for his large family: in total, his two wives bore him twenty children, half of whom survived infancy. (The first wife, his cousin Maria Barbara, died in Anhalt-Cöthen, where he met and married his second wife Anna Magdalena.) Bach was very proud of his family, and in particular of the entire ensemble of musicians he had managed to bring up.

Late in life he started to lose his vision; by 1749 he had gone completely blind, probably due to diabetes (his eye doctor was the same one who treated George Friedrich Handel). In 1750 he died of a stroke.[106] Bach was survived by Anna Magdalena and ten of

---

100 Seaton 311
101 Seaton 312-317
102 Seaton 312
103 Seaton 318
104 Seaton 319
105 Seaton 323
106 Seaton 328

his children.[107] Four of these children, Carl Philip Emanuel, Johann Christian, Philip Emanuel and Johann Christoph Friederich, became more famous musicians in their own lifetimes than their father.[108]

Despite the professional success he had enjoyed during his lifetime, much of Bach's enormous output of music was lost upon his death. He had willed most of his manuscripts to Wilhelm Friedemann Bach, his oldest son, a man who did not value them at their true worth and didn't bother to preserve most of his father's legacy. The works that remain are numbered under the "BWV" system. These letters are an abbreviation for the German "Bachs Werk Verzeichnis," (Bach's Work Catalogue).

Bach spent most of his life trying to find a better job and only ever lived in Thuringia and Saxony, entirely within the bounds of modern Germany.[109] He enjoyed a battle of words, had a good sense of humor (if somewhat coarse) and was very impatient around people who were not as skilled as he was. He was also a very religious man who quietly supported traditional Lutheranism rather than the upstart Pietists.[110] His music is a reflection of these religious leanings, resisting the sentimentality more appropriate to Pietism.

MINUET 1

A minuet is a dance of French origin popular in the 17th and 18th centuries, and an instrumental form derived from its musical accompaniment. The minuet symbolizes more than any other dance the ideals of nonchalance, elegance, subtlety, and nobility of the French court.[111]

---

107 Seaton 328
108 David 24
109 Geck 8
110 David 24
111 Boyd 293

Bach probably did not write the Overture in G Minor BWV 822, which includes Minuet 1 as well as Gavotte in G Minor in Book 3. The real composer is up for speculation.

The minuet itself is a dance using "patterns of four tiny steps set to two bars of music in ¾ time. Several different patterns were normally employed throughout the dance."[112] The partners would be at the opposite ends of a Z shape at the beginning of the dance and would pass each other in the middle as they traced the Z. The true main beat of a minuet is actually every other measure, making the time signature more of a 6/4 beat than ¾.[113] When danced, a minuet was divided into sets of two beats rather than three (step bend / step bend / step step). Dances lasted around 100 measures, so two minuets would have been put together and played over and over again until the dance ended.[114]

MINUETS 2 AND 3

Bach also did not write Minuet 2, BWV 116. It contains similar scales and arpeggio figurations[115] to the work of the Dresden organist and composer Christian Pezold, who definitely did write Minuet 3 (BWV 114) and the entire Minuet in Book 3 (which is a synthesis of two minuets, BWV 114 and 115).[116] In 1717 Bach went to Dresden to challenge a French organist named J. L. Marchand to a composing and improvising duel. Though Marchand did not show up (probably realizing that he was in over his head), we can be glad that Bach went as he probably found Pezold's pieces during that trip.[117] It seems, then, that the Suzuki student's first contact with "the music of Bach" is really more of an encounter with "the music of Christian Pezold and anonymous."

---

112 Boyd 293
113 Boyd 296
114 "Minuet" in Book 3 is an example of two minuets put together. Working on the technical aspect of changing key signatures seems to be the ultimate goal in this particular instance rather than filling out a dance set, giving the student a legitimate argument to eliminate some of the repeats.
115 Bergenfeld 19
116 Bergenfeld 19
117 Bergenfeld 19

We can't be too hard on Bach for what may seem today like egregious copyright theft. During the Baroque era the concept of artistic authorship and originality was different than it is today. In this particular case Bach and his sons put these two minuets into a volume he had compiled in 1725 in order to teach his second wife how to play the keyboard: the *Anna Magdalena Notebook*. Many of the pieces in the book were written by other composers or even his sons, and they are interesting as a study of what the Bach family considered appropriate for pedagogy. Bach probably never meant for the *Notebook* to be published (the cover of the original looks like he used it for scratch paper). Long after his death the desire for all things Bach led to the rediscovery of this volume and its publication under his name, erroneously attributing to him the composition of all, rather than just some of, the pieces in the *Anna Magdalena Notebook*.[118]

ROBERT SCHUMANN
8 June 1810 – 29 July 1856
"Happy Farmer"
Era: Romantic, written 1848
Genre: Piano solo (character piece)

Robert Schumann was born in Saxony and spent most of his life in Leipzig and Dresden. His father, who encouraged his interest in music, died when Schumann was sixteen and his mother convinced him to study law at Leipzig.[119] While there he started taking piano lessons from Friedrich Wieck, with whose daughter Clara he fell in love.[120] Schumann's courtship of Clara has become legendary, in particular because their romance was strongly discouraged by her father (who had to be sued in order to allow the couple to marry).

Schumann eventually ceased his legal studies to become a concert pianist, an ambition that he could never realize due to a finger injury sustained while using his own contraption meant to equalize the use of

---

118 A similar scenario would be the rediscovery 300 years from now of the Suzuki books, and every piece in them attributed to Shinichi Suzuki.
119 Hale 2
120 Hale 2

the fingers.[121] Instead he earned a living writing the *Neue Zeitschrift für Musik*, a magazine which introduced the music of many up-and-coming young composers including Johannes Brahms. He was also an instructor at the Leipzig conservatory and a music director in Düsseldorf.[122] At 23 Schumann showed the first signs of brain disease which led to an unsuccessful attempt to drown himself in the Rhine at the age of 44. He was confined in an asylum for the last two years of his life.[123]

"HAPPY FARMER"

"Happy Farmer" was originally titled: *"Frölicher Landmann, von der Arbeit zurückkehrend"* (The Happy Farmer Coming Home from Work), and comes from Schumann's *Album for the Young*, op. 68.[124] It is marked at MM 116, and should be played *frisch und munter* (in a fresh and lively way). Originally the *Album for the Young*, a set of 43 pieces, was titled *Christmas Album*. "Happy Farmer" is the tenth in the album, and was composed for the birthday of his oldest child.[125]

Schumann had already written many great works, but he was convinced that his small pieces would better stand the test of time. He loved composing opus 68, stating that the pieces had given him "indescribable joy."[126]

FRANÇOIS-JOSEPH GOSSEC
17 January 1734 – 16 February 1829
Gavotte (Also known as *Rosine*)
Era: Classical, written 1786
Genre: Opera

Francois-Joseph Gossec was born in Vergies, Belgium in 1734, and entered a choir school at age six or seven.[127] He studied violin and

---

121 Hale 2
122 Hale 2
123 Hale 2
124 Schumann *Album for the Young, op. 68* 8
125 Bauer
126 Bauer
127 Pitou 250

composition and by 1751 was already conducting an orchestra in Paris (Alexandre Le Riche de La Poupliniere's orchestra,[128] previously led by Jean-Phillipe Rameau and the famous Mannheim composer Johann Stamitz[129]). His rise to fame was helped by Rameau (see Book 6), who gave him this first job and encouraged him to develop symphonies.[130] Gossec was, in fact, the first to compose symphonies in France, a form previously unknown there.[131] Several noble patrons supported Gossec during his early years in Paris, and he also achieved a great deal of popular acclaim. His attempts at writing comic opera, however, were a failure, possibly because of the competition offered by André Gretry (see Book 8). Instead he turned to *tragedie lyrique*, a move also inspired by Rameau.[132] It was during this time that he wrote the opera *Rosine*, from which the Gavotte is taken.

During and after the French Revolution Gossec changed his themes and style to express the will of the people, a move that also led to great success. He "helped create a 'civic music' in which songs, choruses, marches and wind symphonies, designed for outdoor performance by massed forces, served as the voice of the new regime."[133] Gossec became the main force behind the musical propaganda of the Revolution. His career as a composer dwindled with Napoleon Bonaparte's ascension to power in 1799, at which point he became a teacher and wrote books on solfège (a way of teaching music theory).[134][135] After receiving the Legion of Honor from Napoleon,[136] Gossec retired to Passy. Considering the variations of extreme turmoil in France during his ninety-five year lifetime, his knack of being able to adapt and survive were truly extraordinary.

---

128 Pitou 250
129 Brook 186
130 Brook 186
131 Straeten 201
132 Brook 187
133 Brook 188
134 "Solfège," according to the Harvard Dictionary of Music, is the "singing of scales, intervals, and melodic exercises to solmization syllables (do, re, mi, etc.). The term has also been used to encompass all aspects of the teaching of basic music skills; in France particularly, extensive courses of solfège were developed." 793.
135 Brook 188
136 Pitou 250

ROSINE:

Gavotte comes from Gossec's *Rosine*, an opera which generated considerable tumult when it came out on 14 July 1786. It only had six performances before it was dropped from the Paris opera repertory in August of 1786.[137] It tells the story of Germond, who believes that he's been tricked into service with the French army. The whole predicament has been a plan of the servant Delorme to please his master Saint-Fal, who is in love with Germond's wife Rosine. Rosine remains faithful to her husband, however, and spends her time searching for him. In the second act, the plot thickens as Delorme continues to try to separate Rosine and Germond. By the end of the act husband and wife are reunited, and Saint-Fal begins to understand her great love for her husband. In the third act Saint-Fal has decided to let the two alone, and sends Delorme out of the country for his evil ways.[138]

---

137 Pitou 475
138 Pitou 475-6

CHAPTER 2: SUZUKI BOOK 2

GEORGE FRIDERIC HANDEL
23 February 1685 – 14 April 1759
Chorus from *Judas Maccabeus*
Era: Baroque, written 1746
Genre: Oratorio

Georg Friederich Händel (the original spelling of his name) was born in Germany, in the town of Halle. By age seven or eight he was already an accomplished organist.[139] His father, however, had determined that his son would study law. The Duke of Saxe-Weissenfels heard the boy Händel playing the organ and convinced his father to let him work on his music as well (he eventually learned composition, oboe, violin and harpsichord[140]). When Händel was twelve his father died, giving him at once the freedom to choose his profession and also

139 Loft 97
140 Gilder 162

the responsibility of taking care of his family. By age seventeen he was given his first job as an organist. After a year he decided to move away from home and try his hand at writing opera, living first in Hamburg and then Lübeck. When in Lübeck the famous organist Buxtehude retired and the job was offered to Händel - which he might have taken had the offer not been contingent upon marrying Buxtehude's daughter.[141] He then went on to live in various Italian cities, where he became familiar with opera composition.[142]

In 1710 Händel moved to Hannover, where he worked for the Elector, Hannover's hereditary ruler. During this time he went back and forth frequently to London, a city where he appeared to feel more at home than Hannover. The Elector dismissed Händel from service in 1713, presumably for neglecting his post, after which the composer moved to England permanently. The Elector of Hannover eventually moved to London as well, the British laws of succession having turned him into King George I of Great Britain.[143] Happily the composer and the King eventually came to terms. In 1727 Händel became a British subject and changed his name to George Frideric Handel.[144]

Handel's first love was Italian opera, and he opened his own opera company in 1720 in Haymarket (London). This company was very successful until John Gay's *The Beggar's Opera* opened in 1728, a lighter genre of opera that became very popular and which within six months had bankrupted Handel.[145] This disaster, however, led to Handel's greatest achievement as the originator and composer of the English oratorio. The oratorio is a sacred opera which tells a biblical story with a chorus and soloists. There are no staging or costumes, making the oratorio a much less expensive alternative to opera. His first attempt at the genre, *Esther*, was written in 1732.[146] By 1741 Handel was focusing primarily on oratorio instead of opera, a decision that would guarantee his immortality as a composer.[147] Winton Dean writes that:

---

141 Gilder 162
142 Hicks 748
143 Hicks 749
144 Hicks 753
145 Gilder 162
146 Hicks 754
147 Hicks 757

Handel's final achievement, which contributed more than anything else to his lasting fame, was the creation of the English Oratorio. It was a new form, only remotely connected with any of the continental varieties, and his single major innovation. He evolved it by accident, thanks to his reluctance to abandon the theatre, the Bishop of London's intervention against stage performance and middle-class English public's appreciation of familiar Bible stories treated in an epic style that combined entertainment with edification.[148]

From 1737 on Handel was plagued by what the physicians diagnosed as recurring paralysis of the head and hand. In 1751 he started noticing that his eyesight was failing (probably due to cataracts) and by 1753 he had gone completely blind.[149] He died in 1759, and is buried at Westminster Abbey.[150]

CHORUS FROM *JUDAS MACCABEUS*

Judas Maccabeus was written in 1746 and first premiered in Covent Garden in London. The words were written by Dr. Thomas Morell, a clergyman.[151] This oratorio, based on part of First Maccabees, a book in the Apocrypha, tells the story of Hanukkah. In the first act, Judas is at his father's funeral and is appointed leader of the Jewish people. He leads them into battle against their pagan Greek occupiers. In Act II, they have enjoyed some victories but the king of Syria has decided to crush their uprising and destroy the temple in Jerusalem, at that time the center of Jewish worship. Judas goes off into battle again, this time against the king. In Act III, while celebrating the Feast of Lights, the Israelites learn that Judas has routed another huge army. Judas enters and asks the assembled people to eulogize the dead. Then a messenger from the Roman senate comes in, offering independence to Judaea. The oratorio concludes with a hymn for peace.[152]

---

148 Dean *The New Grove Handel* 107
149 Hicks 763
150 Gilder 162
151 "Judas Maccabeus, an Oratorio"
152 Dean *Handel's Dramatic Oratorios and Masques* 464

Chorus from *Judas Maccabeus* comes from Act III, during which a chorus of men and a chorus of women sing "See, the Conqu'ring Hero Comes:"

CHORUS OF YOUTHS:

See the conqu'ring hero comes!
Sound the trumpets, beat the drums.
Sports prepare, the laurel bring,
Songs of triumph to him sing.

CHORUS OF VIRGINS:

See the god-like youth advance!
Breathe the flutes, and lead the dance;
Myrtle wreaths, and roses twine,
To deck the hero's brow divine.[153]

The hero of the song is the returning Judas Maccabeus, triumphantly returning to battle after freeing the Israelites from bondage. An interesting bit of trivia is that Chorus in its original orchestration was the first piece of music to use the snare drum!

Other similar works for listening: *Messiah* (Handel) and *Jeptha* (Handel).

JOHANN SEBASTIAN BACH
Bach: 21 March 1685 – 28 July 1750
Musette
Era: Baroque, written between 1714 and 1719
Genre: Baroque Dance Suite

Musette is from English Suite no. 3 in G Minor, BWV 808, originally one of a set of six English Suites for harpsichord.

---

153 "Judas Maccabeus, An Oratorio"

It was written during Bach's time as concertmaster in Weimar (1714-1717).[154]English Suite no. 3 in G incorporates elements of both French and Italian styles. Bach used these suites as a part of his keyboard curriculum.[155]

For more biographical information on J. S. Bach, see page 11.

CARL MARIA VON WEBER
18 November 1786 – 5 June 1826
"Hunter's Chorus"
Era: Romantic, written 1817-1821
Genre: Opera

Carl Maria von Weber was born to an extraordinary and somewhat eccentric family. His father Franz Anton Weber was first a city musician and then the leader of a traveling theater company. Franz decided at some point that he would become an aristocrat and took the name Franz Anton von Weber. (The word "von" in a German last name indicates nobility and is usually not self-created.) Carl Maria is known historically as a "von Weber" only as a result of habit and not from any genuine ennoblement.[156] Another of his relatives, his first cousin Constanze Weber, became famous as the wife of Wolfgang Amadeus Mozart.[157] The family in general was inclined toward both music and excess.

Weber grew up traveling with his father's troupe, learning music along the way despite ill health and a chronic limp. Franz Anton, noting the Mozart family's profits in the child prodigy line, tried to force young Carl into the same business.[158] His first teacher was his stepbrother, followed by Michael Hayden, J. N. Kalcher and

---

154 Wolff 147

155 Wolff 330

156 The usage of "von" was supposed to be the exclusive right of nobles, distinguishing them from commoners. Of the "von" composers in the Suzuki books only one was actually an aristocrat. The "van" in Ludwig van Beethoven's name is Dutch, and didn't necessarily signify nobility. Karl Ditters von Dittersdorf was born Karl Ditters, but legitimately acquired "von" when he was ennobled in order to fulfill a requirement for one of his jobs.

157 Randel 968

158 Warrack 30

eventually Abbé Vogler.[159] It was through Abbé Vogler that Weber became enamored of all things exotic, folk song, and the idea of the unspoiled country rustic (all three are tendencies which characterize the Romantic philosopher and artist).[160] Weber wrote his first opera at thirteen and would eventually become music director of opera houses, first in Prague and then in Dresden.[161] Weber's true talent as an opera composer lay in infusing stock heroic characters with a real sense of personality.[162]

Carl's life was substantially affected by his father's eccentricities. For example, an employer once entrusted Carl with a large sum of money with which to purchase a horse. Franz Anton, wandering by, saw the money, took it and put it toward paying off his many debts. Carl was eventually banished from his employer's lands as a result. Franz Anton was also responsible for the end of Carl's singing career. Carl came home from directing an opera one evening, saw an open wine bottle on the table, and took a drink. He didn't know that his father had emptied the bottle of wine and filled it with acid for his lithography experiments. Carl barely survived the incident, and his voice was never the same.

Der Freischütz, or *The Free Shooter*, was one of Carl's foremost successes. Written in 1821, it was a combination of the old fashioned German *Singspiel* (dialogue is both spoken and sung, for example W. A. Mozart's *Zauberflöte*) and something new: it was the first major German Romantic opera. *Der Freischütz* combined folk tunes and intense musical drama that foreshadowed the artistry of Richard Wagner.[163] It was an instant hit and still packs opera houses to this day.

"HUNTER'S CHORUS"

"Hunter's Chorus" comes from *Der Freischütz*. As the opera begins, a young man, Max, loses a shooting contest to a peasant. He begins to fear that he will be unable to win the next day's contest, the outcome of which will decide who will marry his beloved Agathe (the

---

159 Ewen 408
160 Warrack *Carl Maria von Weber* 57
161 Ewen 408
162 Warrack *Carl Maria von Weber* 43
163 Ewen 409

daughter of the head forester). Max has a friend Kaspar who offers to get him some magic bullets. These bullets will always hit the target. Unfortunately Max must go to the Wolf's Glen to make a deal with the evil demon Samiel in order to get the magic bullets (*Freikugel*). Samiel agrees to make the bullets with the caveat (known only to Kaspar) that the last bullet will go where Samiel, rather than Max, directs. This scene in the Wolf's Glen is one of the more famous in opera, with the forging of each of the bullets creating an even more terrifying musical image: "first flapping woodbirds, secondly a black boar, thirdly a violent storm, fourth the cracking of whips and trampling of horses and fiery wheels, fifth the Wild Hunt, sixth thunder, lightning, torrential rain, will-o'-the wisps and fire from earth, and seventh Samiel himself."[164]

The next day is the contest. Agathe is wearing her wedding dress in preparation, but is disturbed when a box, which should contain her wedding flowers, contains a funeral wreath instead. Meanwhile Ottokar, prince of the realm, is listening to his huntsmen sing the Chorus of Huntsmen, the song that will be familiar to Suzuki students as the "Hunter's Chorus:"[165]

What pleasure on earth can compare with the hunter's?
Whose cup of life sparkles so richly?
To lie in the verdure while the horns sound,
To follow the stag through thicket and pond,
Is joy for a prince, is a real man's desire,
It strengthens your limbs and spices your food.
When woods and rocks resound all about us,
A full goblet sings a freer and happier song!
Yo ho! Tralala!
Diana is present to brighten the night;
Her darkness cools us like any refreshment in the day.
To fell the bloody wolf, and the boar
Who greedily roots through the green crops,

---

164 Warrack 12-13

165 Weber's inspiration for his male choruses probably came from gatherings of quasi-secret societies which would get together and discuss music, art and literature. His particular group was called *Faust's Hollenfahrt*, and his secret code name was *Krautsalat*, or "Cabbage Salad." Warrack *Carl Maria von Weber* 68.

Is joy for a prince, is real man's desire,
It strengthens your limbs and spices your food.
When woods and rocks resound all about us,
A full goblet sings a freer and happier song!
Yo, ho! Tralala![166]

At the contest the bullet that is meant to hit Agathe is deflected and hits Kaspar instead. The prince finds out about the magic bullet scheme and very nearly banishes Max. Instead a Hermit intervenes, and the prince allows Max to marry Agathe in a year's time without banishment. The opera ends with a chorus of praise for God's mercy.[167]

THOMAS HAYNES BAYLY
1797- 22 April 1839
Long, Long Ago
Era: Romantic, published 1843
Genre: Song

For information on *Long, Long Ago* and Thomas Haynes Bayly, see page 6.

JOHANNES BRAHMS
7 May 1833- 3 April 1897
Waltz
Era: Romantic, written 1865
Genre: 4 hands piano music: Op. 39-5 in E Major

---

166 Libretto from Der Freischutz, 64-5
167 Ewen 410-11

Johannes Brahms was born in Hamburg to a musical but poor family. His father, who played double bass, was his first teacher.[168] When he was only fourteen Brahms had to start earning a living in order to help out his family, which he did by playing piano in disreputable taverns.[169] Legend has it that disillusionment caused by this work kept him from ever marrying.

By age twenty Brahms secured himself a different job, this time as accompanist to the violinist Eduard Remenyi. It was through Remenyi that Brahms met Robert and Clara Schumann, friends who would eventually bring about his rise to fame through articles in the periodical *Neue Zeitschrift fuer Musik*.[170] (Brahms' love of Clara Schumann is still fueling the rumor mills of music history because, lamentably, no one has ever been able to pinpoint the exact nature of their relationship.) Brahms worked in several different cities between 1857 and 1863, after which he settled in Vienna, where he would remain for the rest of his life.[171] He eventually became very successful as a composer, garnering honor after honor.[172]

Brahms was a giant of western musical composition. He was one of the first to look back to past forms and use them for contemporary compositions, merging an intellectual approach to music with the lyricism of song. Fans of Richard Wagner were his chief rivals, insisting that music be programmatic (that is, follow some dramatic storyline).[173] Despite opposition Brahms continued to compose what is known as "absolute music," music devoted to form and an abstract ideal of beauty.

WALTZ

Waltz was originally written as a piano piece for four hands and was a part of a collection titled Waltzes for Piano. It was dedicated to the music critic Eduard Hanslick.[174] Though it was written in 1865, it was first performed in Hamburg on 15 November 1867.

---

168 Ewen 675
169 Ewen 675
170 Ewen 675
171 Ewen 675
172 Ewen 675
173 Ewen 673
174 Bozarth 184

1865 was a significant year for Brahms. In February his mother died, and shortly afterword he started writing the *German Requiem*.[175] Due to financial problems, beginning in 1865 and continuing for the next four years he had to "undertake lengthy concert tours in Germany, Switzerland, Austria, Hungary, Denmark and the Netherlands. . ."[176] Though these other events may seem more monumental in scope, it was through pieces such as the Opus 39 Waltzes that Brahms created a name for himself as a composer for amateurs.[177]

GEORGE FRIDERIC HANDEL
23 February 1685 – 14 April 1759
Bourrée
Era: Baroque, written perhaps in 1711/2
Genre: Sonata for Flute and Continuo

This Bourrée is the fourth movement of the Sonata in G Major for Flute and Basso Continuo, Opus 1, No. 5 (HWV 363b). It was published as a part of the same collection as the violin sonatas (see Books 6 and 7). The full title of the work was "*SOLOS For a GERMAN FLUTE a HOBOY or VIOLIN With a Thorough Bass for the HARPSICHORD or BASS VIOLIN, Opera Prima.*" Its first publication was pirated and appeared in a work that included some sonatas definitely written by Handel and some that were probably not. This Bourrée was possibly written by Handel. If it was his composition, it was probably written during his time in Hannover between 1711 and 1712.[178] It is possible that this work was written for oboe rather than the flute.[179] There are several manuscript fragments of this piece in different keys.

For more biographical information on Handel see the entry on Chorus from *Judas Maccabeus* on page 19.

---

175 Bozarth 184
176 Bozarth 184
177 Bozarth 184
178 Schmitz V
179 Hicks 802

ROBERT SCHUMANN
8 June 1810 – 29 July 29 1856
"The Two Grenadiers"
Era: Romantic, written 1840
Genre: Lied (Song)

"The Two Grenadiers," Op. 49, No. 1 is from Schumann's collection *Romances and Ballads*, vol. II, and was originally a song that he wrote to the words of a ballad by the great romantic poet Heinrich Heine. The piece was composed in 1840 along with more than 120 other similar works, a period that he called his "Year of Song."[180] He was, at the time, still trying to sue Clara Wieck's father into letting him marry her.[181] Some of the songs, this one included, seem to reflect either the tragedy of his situation or just tragedy in general.

"The Two Grenadiers" in its original form is quite a bit longer than the piece in Suzuki Book 2. Suzuki is following a time-honored tradition when he arranges a song to be a solo for an instrument other than the voice, a practice that "is nearly as old as western music itself."[182] Though this rendering transforms the song into something more abstract, knowledge of its impassioned lyrics lend drama to an instrumental interpretation:

To France were faring two Grenadiers,
From prison in Russia returning,
And when they came to the German frontiers,
Their heads they did hang in mourning;
For there they were met by the tidings of fear,
That France in her power was shaken,
Defeated, destroy'd was the army so dear,
And the Emp'ror, the Emp'ror was taken.

Then wept they together the Grenadiers,
To hear such news on returning!
And then one said: "'Tis death that nears,

---

180 Burkholder 611
181 Burkholder 611
182 Gibbs 224

Like fire my old wound is burning!"
The other said: "the end has come,
No longer life I cherish!;
But I've a wife and child at home,
Without me they must perish."

"Who cares for child, who cares for wife!
New hope in my heart shall awaken!
Let them go and beg if they care for life,
My Emp'ror, my Emp'ror is taken!

I pray thee, Brother, for a boon;
I feel, my hour is coming,
Oh! Carry my body to France again,
In France I would rest from roaming.
The cross of honor that I wear,
Here on my heart thou'lt bind me,
And lay my gun beside me there,
And gird my sword around me.

(Marseillaise)
Alert and still in my grave, array'd
Like a sentinel I'll be lying,
Until I hear to the loud cannonade
The neigh of the chargers replying.
Then 'twill be the Emp'ror that rides o'er my grave,
And swords are flashing and falling,
And swords are flashing and falling!
All ready and arm'd I'll arise from the grave,
The Emp'ror, the Emp'ror is calling![183]

Schumann was one of the first to believe that the voice (or, in our case, violin) and the piano should have equal importance in song.[184] In "The Two Grenadiers" both parts are integral to the plot of the poem, giving an even greater intensity to Heine's words. He used the French

---

183 Schumann *Vocal Album: Fifty-five Songs for Low Voice* 134-139
184 Burkholder 611

national anthem, the *Marseillase*, at the end of the piece to rouse the emotions into a frenzy, apparently a habit of his (he used the it in two other songs).[185] The extreme emotions and abundant national fervor of this piece make it a good example of Romanticism in music.

For more biographical information on Schumann see the entry on "Happy Farmer"on page 15.

NICCOLÒ PAGANINI
27 October 1782 – 27 May 1840
Theme from *Witches Dance*
Era: Romantic, written in 1813
Genre: Theme and Variations

Niccolò Paganini was among the most notorious virtuosos in violin history. He had a difficult start in life: at five years old he went into a catatonic state after an illness and was only saved from being buried alive by twitching in his shroud during his wake. It was after this ominous event that Paganini started his violin lessons. His father, who had an insignificant job at a shipping company,[186] was his first teacher and, by all reports, not a very benevolent man. He understood his son's potential as a virtuoso and chose to foster it by severe punishments for mistakes, insisting on incessant practicing, beatings and even starvation to keep him to task. [187] Paganini eventually went on to other teachers, though most of them worked with him only briefly. He achieved his first significant success as a soloist at the cathedral in Genoa, where he was required to play a new concerto each week.[188] At age fifteen he had started touring,[189] and by the time he turned twenty-eight Paganini was considered Italy's greatest violinist.[190]

In 1822 at age thirty Paganini was diagnosed with syphilis. Its treatment, a cocktail of mercury and opium, made him into a gaunt and

---

185 Gibbs 236
186 Kenyon
187 Stratton 6
188 Kenyon
189 Stratton 13
190 Randel 662

31

mysterious figure.[191] He garnered a reputation for demonic wildness and a total lack of morals, probably due to his one-sided education.[192] Paganini's maturity as a violinist grew through the years, and by his forties he had toured Milan, Paris, Vienna, Venice and London with great success.[193] Most of Europe had fallen at his feet. In later years his popularity waned due to reports of his greediness.[194] Even after his death Paganini was a controversial figure, not allowed a burial for five years and then exhumed fifty years later "in order that his features might once more be gazed upon."[195]

Despite his formal training as a child, Paganini was a virtuoso who liked to think of himself as self-taught. Certainly as a violinist he was an original. His technique was, in many ways, uniquely his own.[196] One of his more radical inventions was his idea of pieces for one or two strings, compositions which offended some people and inspired a host of copycats.[197] He composed mostly for the violin, works which include a set of twenty-four caprices and six violin concertos.[198] The 24 Caprices are now a standard of the violin repertoire and their mastery is considered essential for the aspiring violinist.

THEME FROM *WITCHES' DANCE*

Theme from *Witches' Dance* is an excerpt from a much longer work: *Le Streghe (The Witches)*, Op. 8 MS 19. The theme itself was originally in the *Witches' Dance* from the ballet *Le Nozze di Benevento*, composed by Franz Xavier Sussmayer and premiered in 1802. Paganini took the theme and expanded it into what he called *Comic dances of the Witches under the walnut tree of Beneveto, composed and performed by Signor Paganini*.[199] The piece that is in Book

---

191 Randel 662
192 Stratton 14
193 Kenyon
194 Randel 662
195 Stratton 4
196 Randel 662
197 Randel 662
198 Randel 662
199 Stratton 167

2 is hinted at in Paganini's work but never played in its entirety and should, in fact, be considered a composition of Sussmayer's.

The complete *Le Streghe* is a set of variations on the Sussmayer theme, some of which are almost impossibly difficult to play (most of the piece is only appropriate for the student who has surpassed Book 10). *Le Streghe* is a testimony to Paganini's desire to write pieces only meant for his own use: music that contributed to his mystique and was too difficult for anyone else. Nicholas Kenyon writes that:

> This piece sums up all that listeners found most irresistible about Paganini's talent: its diabolic programme and fierce exploitation of the violin's every possibility provided them with an opportunity to fantasize about Paganini as a messenger from the devil himself.[200]

AMBROISE THOMAS
5 August 1811- 12 February 1896
Gavotte from *Mignon*
Era: Romantic, written 1866
Genre: Opera

Ambroise Thomas started studying at the Paris Conservatory at seventeen, and only four years later won the prestigious Prix de Rome. While at the Conservatory he composed chamber music, songs, a requiem mass and various other works. By 1834 he had obtained an introduction to the *Opéra-Comique* with his one-act operetta *La Double Echelle*, after which he successfully wrote a number of operas and *opéra-comiques*.[201] At fifty-five he became the director of the Paris Conservatory.[202]

Thomas wrote *Mignon* in 1866 after a six-year decline in popularity. *Mignon* is an opera based on J. W. von Goethe's *Wilhelm Meister's Apprenticeship* (1795). Thomas thought that it would surely fail to gain much attention but, much to his surprise, it "turned out to be one of those works that make the fortune of both the opera

---

200 Kenyon
201 Biancolli 499
202 Guilder 347

and the theater."[203] Because of this opera he was the first composer to live long enough to see one of his own works' 1000th performance.[204] (Gavotte from *Mignon* was played at the gala the following day![205]) Some of the qualities that endeared *Mignon* to the public were its "clear, correct, melodious and elegantly expressive music – a splendid example of those eminently French qualities as descended from the eighteenth century through the line of Monsigny, Gretry and Boieldieu."[206]

At the end of his life Thomas became very introspective, obsessed with the idea of death. He died in Paris, and his funeral was well attended. Massenet gave an eloquent oration.[207]

THE STORY OF *MIGNON*[208]

As *Mignon* begins, a mad singer enters a German tavern looking for his long-lost daughter. Meanwhile the girl Mignon is refusing to do the egg-dance (something that the gypsy chief Giarno wants her to do). The student Wilhelm Meister draws his pistol in her defense and buys her, and subsequently she falls in love with him. Wilhelm and Mignon leave with Filena (an actress) and her troupe to go to a castle, where he plans to fill the role of poet. When Mignon realizes that Wilhelm is in love with someone else (Filena) she decides to drown herself. On her way to the river she runs into the mad singer and tells him that she wishes the castle would be destroyed by lightening. The singer, taking her literally, goes off and immediately sets fire to the castle. Filena hurries out of the burning building, on her way telling Mignon that she left behind a bouquet of flowers that Wilhelm gave her. Mignon rushes in to save the flowers and ends up being rescued again by Wilhelm. The mad singer suddenly regains his reason and realizes that he is actually the Count Cipriani, the castle is his, and Mignon is his daughter!

---

203 Biancolli 500
204 Biancolli 500
205 Biancolli 500
206 Grout *A Short History of Opera* 399
207 Biancolli 500
208 Though it is difficult to believe, for an opera *Mignon* does not have an unusually fantastic plotline.

Wilhelm discovers that he's in love with Mignon, not Filena, and they all live happily ever after.[209]

JEAN-BAPTISTE LULLY
(MARIN MARAIS, 1656-1728)
29 November 1632 – 22 March 1687
Gavotte
Era: Baroque, 1686

> This adroit manipulator did succeed in becoming the virtual dicta-
> tor of French musical life, but he became more than that: a mighty
> force to contend with not only in France but wherever there was
> a serious musical culture. For this masterful intrigant was also a
> great artist, and in that capacity he remained uncompromising and
> absolutely true to his vocation.[210]

Jean-Baptiste Lully was the epitome of the French composer, though, surprisingly, he was born and raised in Italy. He seemed to be able to pick up any skill: as a child he learned to play the violin and guitar (probably self-taught[211]), as well as becoming a proficient acro-bat and dancer.[212] As a fourteen-year-old Lully moved to France to be the tutor to one of the King's cousins, a very high-ranking aristocrat named Anne Marie Louise d'Orleans.[213] When his skills as a musician

---

209 Biancolli 501-2
210 Heyer 2
211 Bachmann 376
212 Gorce 292
213 Scott 12

and dancer were discovered he became a popular member of her little orchestra.[214] Lully rapidly ascended the social ladder in his adopted country, going from language tutor to head musician for the King of France in a period of fifteen years.[215]

Lully was best known for his ballets and operas, and his love of spectacle led to a distinct style of fantastic composition which became synonymous with French opera. Eventually he acquired a sort of musical monopoly: "he purchased a royal privilege granting him the exclusive right to produce sung drama in France."[216] In other words, no one else was allowed to write opera. Lully died from gangrene, an injury he sustained while conducting an orchestra. (During Lully's lifetime "conducting" was merely pounding a staff-like baton on the floor in time with the beat. His mistake was to miss the floor and accidently gouge his foot.) His influence was so great that his early death left a hole in the French music scene that would not be filled until the time of Rameau (See page 75).[217]

MARIN MARAIS

Lully, though a pivotal figure in western music, is not actually represented in the Suzuki books. Gavotte was written by the French gambist Marin Marais (1656-1728).[218] Marais, who was born the son of a Parisian shoemaker and started his musical career as a choirboy, eventually became a "central figure in the French school of viola da gamba players that flourished in Paris in the late 17th and early 18th centuries."[219] He was very briefly a student of Sainte-Columbe, the leading viol player of his day. Sainte-Columbe was so afraid that Marais would surpass him that he refused to teach him after six months of instruction. Not to be deterred, Marais hid where he could listen to and steal Sainte-Columbe's secret practicing techniques.[220]

---

214 Scott 25
215 Gorce 293
216 Burkholder 358
217 Scott 9
218 Wissick 46
219 Wissick 46
220 Hsu xiii

Marais was appointed to Louis XIV as court gambist in 1679 and studied composition with Lully. Marais' style as a composer was more French than Italian – that is, more refined and less expressive.[221] As well as being one of the king's favorite chamber musicians, Marais was a well-regarded teacher.[222] One of the things he asked of all his students was that they review all of his compositions once every two weeks, a habit which should sound familiar to Suzuki students![223]

It's hard to tell why this particular piece was eventually attributed to Lully. One guess is that the book's dedication to Lully, which was written in big letters on the front page, led to the case of mistaken identity. Another speculation is that Lully, "ruthless in his desire to control his competitors,"[224] gave himself credit for its authorship.

GAVOTTE

Gavotte is a rondeau from the opening suite in Book I of pieces for gamba and basso continuo by Marais. The Rondeau in Marais' book is very similar to the one in the Suzuki book, though it has more ornamentation and several more measures.

Gavotte has the traditional gavotte dance form, that is, four beat measures with the piece starting on beat three. During Marais' time tempos had not yet been standardized, but typically they would have been moderate. A gavotte, for example, would run about mm 80 to the half note.[225] (For a more comprehensive definition of a gavotte, see Gavotte in G Minor on page 45.) With the possible exceptions of the folk tunes, this is the oldest piece in the Suzuki books.

LUDWIG VAN BEETHOVEN
17 December 1770 – 26 March 1827
Minuet in G, WoO 10
Era: Classical, 1795
Genre: Pianoforte

---

221 Hsu xvi
222 Hsu xiv
223 Hsu xiv
224 Wissick 46
225 Hsu xxiv

Ludwig van Beethoven came from a musical family: both his father and his grandfather were musicians in Bonn, though his father was considered the most mediocre of the three generations.[226] Beethoven was the oldest of three brothers. He was only a teenager when his mother died and his father descended into crippling alcoholism, at which point Ludwig had to provide for his family.

Before his mother died Beethoven had traveled to Vienna. While there he met Wolfgang Amadeus Mozart and resolved to study composition with him. Beethoven's mother's illness forced him to return to Bonn before he could seriously enter into a course of instruction with the young composer. It was unfortunately two years before he could return to Vienna to take a job as a court musician, during which time Mozart had died. Instead, Beethoven took lessons with Joseph Haydn, lessons which lasted a full year despite Beethoven's later assertion that he had learned nothing.[227] He subsequently took lessons with Johann Georg Albrechtsberger and Antonio Salieri.[228]

Possibly because he was still supporting his two brothers in Bonn, or perhaps because the cost of living was high in Vienna, Beethoven needed to earn more than his court musician's stipend. To that end he turned to showing off his skill as a piano virtuoso and composer. He quickly became successful in both areas. Beethoven never went back to Bonn, taking up residence in Vienna for the rest of his life. Eventually his brothers followed him there, and they continued to be

---

226 Kerman 73
227 Kerman 76
228 Salieri became famous in the movie *Amadeus* as W. A. Mozart's nemesis.

close as a family (though inclined to intense conflict, even to the point of blows in the street).

In his personal life Beethoven suffered two major tragedies: his deafness, which started gradually at the age of 31 and increased through the years until he was unable to hear anything at all,[229] and his tendency to fall in love with women either too young for him or of higher social class. Despite the deafness Beethoven continued composing and playing throughout his life. He never did marry, though he longed for a family of his own and eventually became the legal guardian of his nephew Karl. Beethoven's relations with his two sisters-in-law were always difficult. He tried to jail his brother Johann's wife and successfully took his brother Caspar's widow to court in order to take her son Karl from her. Beethoven's relationships with family, friends and patrons were almost always dramatic. His personality seemed to either repel the people around him or draw them in. Like Bach, Beethoven was contemptuous of most of his fellow composers and musicians.

Professionally Beethoven was one of the most pivotal figures in the history of music. His early career as a composer was firmly in the Classical style, though later he would open the way for the Romantics. Until Beethoven, composers had to publish enormous amounts or find other jobs. Mozart and Bach's prolific output is touted as a wonder today; in their time, however, composing quickly was more a matter of survival than virtuosity. Though it is true that Beethoven composed a tremendous number of pieces, he took far more time with each one than was the case for his forbears. Unlike previous composers his symphonies numbered nine, not in the hundreds. He revised and rewrote extensively. Beethoven was allowed this luxury because of a generous stipend given to him by three noblemen, a stipend which paid for a comfortable living regardless of how much he wrote.

Historians usually divide his works into three periods: the first was one of imitation, during which time he conformed for the most part to the conventions of Classical composition.[230] The second period becomes more interesting: in 1800, Beethoven made what he called a "fresh start," during which time his music became a "reflection of the changes taking place, a conflict with society and the status quo,

---

229 Kerman 80
230 Ewen 289

a necessity to communicate ideas and ideals, a seeking out of new techniques, idioms and forms."[231] This period is what became generally known as his "expressive" phase. David Ewen suggests that Beethoven's deafness was also partially responsible for his breakthroughs in composition: exiled from the world of sound around him, he created his own, one which discarded convention and spoke with his own personal voice.[232] At the end of his life is the "reflective" period, one which combined new forms with an even more spiritualized concept of music.[233] It was during this time that his Symphony no. 9 was composed, famous for its musical setting of Friedrich Schiller's "Ode to Joy."

MINUET IN G

This name of this minuet in its entirety is: Minuet in G No. 2, WoO 10. It is a part of a group of six minuets that was written in 1795, during Beethoven's Classical period, and was probably originally scored for orchestra.[234] Beethoven had just stopped taking lessons from Haydn and had moved on to instruction in counterpoint with Albrechtsberger. He had not yet started to become deaf, at which later stage he would break out of the mold to become what we think of now as a composer in the Romantic style.

The "WoO" stands for *Werke ohne Opuszahl*, or "works without opus number." Beethoven was stingy with his opus numbers, especially at the time. He wanted his official publications to make a sensation, and the year that the Minuet in G was written the only work to which he assigned an opus number was a set of three piano trios.[235] The trios did make him a great deal of money. This little minuet, however, despite its humble beginnings, has become one of the better-known pieces of the Classical repertoire. Minuet in G also plays a prominent role in the musical *The Music Man*.

---

231 Ewen289
232 Ewen 289
233 Ewen 289
234 Kerman 77
235 Kerman 77

LUIGI BOCCHERINI
19 February 1743- 28 May 1805
Minuet
Era: Classical, written 1771
Genre: string quintet

Luigi Boccherini was born in Lucca, Italy, and was taught to play the cello by his father. He eventually acquired fame as a musician, performing and composing in Rome, Vienna, Prussia, and Paris before settling down in Madrid at age twenty-six.[236] During his sixteen years in Madrid Boccherini was employed by Don Luis, the brother of the king.[237] Between 1785 and 1787 he was a chamber musician at the court of Frederick William II in Prussia, and then he moved back to Madrid. Boccherini died in obscurity and poverty in 1805.[238]

Boccherini is credited with bringing the viola and the cello into greater prominence in chamber music, not surprising considering that he was himself acclaimed as a cello virtuoso.[239] His quintets are more often than not scored for two cellos rather than two violas. Boccherini's major output was chamber music: in total he wrote 125 string quintets and 100 string quartets, as well as multiple symphonies and works for the cello.[240] He was also a significant force in the development of sonata form.[241] (For a definition of "sonata form" see "Back to the Basics" on page xxv.)

MINUET

Minuet is from Boccherini's String Quintet in E Major, Op. 13 no. 5 (scored for two violins, viola and two cellos). It was written in 1771, shortly after Boccherini started working at the court of Don Luis.[242] In the original, this movement is played by two muted violins while the

---

236 Loft 218
237 Ewen 284
238 Ewen 284
239 Ewen 284
240 Randel 88
241 Ewen 284
242 Miyama 4

other three instruments play pizzicato.[243] In 1771 the composer cata-
logued it as a part of his Opus 11, but when it was published four years
later it was renamed Opus 13.[244]

Critical opinion indicates an ambivalence almost approaching dis-
like for Minuet. David Ewen writes about the Minuet that "it is truly
ironical that a composer who wrote as much as Boccherini did – and
often so well – should be known to so many music lovers almost ex-
clusively through [this] charming trifle."[245] Yoshio Miyama writes that
Minuet was not popular during the composer's lifetime but "seems to
have suddenly become famous in Paris in the middle of the 1870s, for
what reason is not known."[246] It might be interesting to try listening to
or playing some of Boccherini's other works, which will probably give
the Suzuki student an entirely different idea of the composer's style!

---

243 Miyama 4
244 Miyama 4
245 Ewen 284
246 Miyama 4

CHAPTER 3: SUZUKI BOOK 3

(PADRE) GIOVANNI BATTISTA MARTINI
24 April 1706 – 3 August 1784
Gavotte
Era: Baroque/Classical published in 1742
Genre: Baroque Dance Suite

Giovanni Battista Martini (called "Padre" Martini, hence the "P" in the Suzuki Book) was one of the most influential musicians of the eighteenth century. As a child he learned about music from his father, a violinist, and had an avid curiosity about other fields such as mathematics.[247] At fifteen Martini decided that he wanted to become a monk and was sent to a Franciscan convent in Lugo di Romagna.[248] In 1725 he accepted the position as *maestro di cappella* in San Francisco, Bologna, and was ordained a priest in 1729.[249] Martini devoted much of his time to composing, writing and teaching. Though he traveled a little through Italy and had numerous offers in more prestigious places, he lived in Bologna with the same job for the rest of his life.[250] At the time, Bologna was considered one of the most important music centers in Europe.

Padre Martini's letters and his library have been extremely useful to historians trying to piece together the history of music during the eighteenth century. Six thousand of his letters survive, some of them

---

247 Kuhn 2310
248 Brofsky 921
249 Brofsky 921
250 Borofsky 921

43

from very well known members of the musical community: Locatelli, Burney, Gretry, Quantz, Rameau and Tartini were among his correspondents.[251] Scholars, kings and popes also wrote to Padre Martini.[252] He collected books from around Europe (the music critic Charles Burney estimated that he had 17,000 volumes by the year 1770, a tremendous number for that day and age[253]). Later this library would become the foundation for the Civic Musical Library in Bologne.[254] His famous pupils included J.C. Bach, Gretry and W.A. Mozart. As a twenty-year-old, Mozart once wrote to Martini that "I never cease to grieve that I am far away from that one person in the world whom I love, revere and esteem above all."[255]

GAVOTTE

Gavotte is the last movement of Martini's Sonata no. 12 for harpsichord, published in Amsterdam in 1742.[256] Over half of his published works were sonatas for either harpsichord or organ. It is difficult to say if it fits into the Classical or Baroque style. Martini's works fall into the time spans of both, and are prime examples of the very real continuity between the Baroque and Classical eras. Gavotte seems to be a part of the Classical *galant* tradition. A piece that is *galant* is light, graceful and refined.[257]

**ATTRIBUTED TO JOHANN SEBASTIAN BACH
(WRITTEN BY CHRISTIAN PEZOLD)**
21 March 1685 – 28 July 1750
Minuet
Era: Baroque, around 1717
Genre: Baroque Dance Suite

---

251 Borofsky 922
252 Kuhn 2310
253 Borofsky 922
254 Kuhn 2310
255 Borofsky 921
256 Robison LP cover
257 Heartz 431

Minuet contains two separate minuets: BWV 114 and BWV 115. Both of them were originally written by the Dresden organist Christian Pezold and then borrowed in Bach's instructional book to his second wife, the *Anna Magdalena Notebook*. Shinichi Suzuki combined the two pieces, which is actually what a Baroque performer would have done when playing them for a dance. (One minuet alone does not take up enough time.) As previously stated in the chapter on Book 1, Bach did not steal these pieces maliciously in order to take fame and glory from Pezold. The *Notebook* was probably never meant to be published under Bach's name; rather, the pieces within seemed to serve as a collection of Bach's pedagogically preferred compositions.

For more information on the biography of Bach and the Minuets see page 11.

JOHANN SEBASTIAN BACH
21 March 1685 – 28 July 1750
Gavotte in G Minor
Era: Baroque
Genre: Baroque Dance Suite

The Gavotte is a dance performed with various different types of steps and music at least from the 1580s to the 1790s. It was especially well known as a French court dance from the courts of Louis XIV and XV, where it was frequently enjoyed in theatrical works and as a social dance. Both music and dance achieved widespread popularity during the pastoral craze of the 1720s to 1730s, when it was favored because of the predictable rhyme of its balanced phrases. It was during this period that Bach wrote most of his gavottes.[258]

A gavotte characteristically has an eight bar phrase[259] and begins on beat three of a four beat time signature. Most of the gavottes written by Bach in the Suzuki books are French, that is, moderate in emotion

---

258 Boyd 187
259 Boyd 187

and predictable in balance.[260] (The Italian gavotte, on the other hand, is more virtuosic.)

This particular gavotte was published as a movement in the Overture in G Minor BWV 822, originally for keyboard. Within the same overture is a minuet that we know in the Suzuki repertoire by the name Minuet 1. Probably neither of these pieces was originally written by Bach, but they were copied down by his hand sometime before 1707.

For more biographical information on Johann Sebastian Bach see page 11.

ANTONÍN DVOŘÁK
8 September 1841 – 1 May 1904
Humoresque
Era: Romantic, written 1894
Genre: Piano piece

Antonín Dvořàk was born in Bohemia to a moderately musical but unsophisticated Czech family.[261] Recognizing Antonín's potential, his parents went to considerable sacrifice to ensure that their son received a good musical education.[262] Dvořàk went on to be a professional string and piano performer, a teacher and a composer. He toured much of Europe, garnering more praise outside of his native land than within it (due for the most part to politics).[263] In 1892 Dvořàk took a job in New York at the National Conservatory of Music.[264] While there he wrote his "New World" Symphony. Due to a recession he returned to Bohemia in 1895 and spent the rest of his life in his native land. During these final years he wrote several operas, including *Rusalka*.

Dvořàk is best known for his interest in native music. Many of his works reflect his own Czech heritage. While in the United States he was fascinated by African and Native American music. He commented once that

---

260 Boyd 187
261 Bohlin 777
262 Bohlin 778
263 Bohlin 781
264 Bohlin 783

[T]he plantation songs are indeed the most striking and appealing melodies that have yet been found on this side of the water. . . Undoubtedly the germs for the best in music lie hidden among all the races that are commingled in this great country. The music of the people is like a rare and lovely flower growing amidst encroaching weeds. Thousands pass it, while others trample it under foot, and thus the chances are that it will perish before it is seen by the one discriminating spirit who will prize it above all else. The fact that no one has as yet arisen to make the most of it does not prove that nothing is there.[265]

Dvořàk was appalled by most Americans' neglect for their own grassroots music. He encouraged students of various backgrounds to share their talents and unique ideas. Recently in the United States there has been a surge of interest in all things non-Western, so this concept should be nothing new to the contemporary student. Dvořàk, however, had the distinction of encouraging cultural diversity in music before it was popularly acceptable.

HUMORESQUE, OP. 101, NO. 7

This piece was originally written for piano and was the seventh in the piano anthology *8 Humoresques*.[266] It was written in 1894, that is, while he was still employed in the United States. Thus Humoresque is the only piece in the Suzuki repertoire composed outside of Europe (with the exception of Dr. Suzuki's own compositions).[267] The idea for Humoresque probably came from a composition of one of Dvořàk's American students, Maurice Arnold Strothotte. The second movement of Arnold's *American Plantation Dances* contains a "lilting skipping dance for solo clarinet, striking because it reminds everyone of the celebrated Humoresque no. 7. . . They share the same gavotte rhythm, phrase lengths, and plagal cadences. . . It predates Humoresque no. 7 by a year and was probably its inspiration."[268] It is not known whether

---

265 Burkholder 745
266 Bohlin 805
267 Bohlin 784
268 Peress 46

or not Arnold was black, but he was definitely an enthusiastic supporter of African-American music and did his best to incorporate it into all of his compositions.

At the beginning of the twentieth century Humoresque no. 7 was extremely popular (it is frequently preceded by the word "ubiquitous"). Fritz Kreisler arranged a fantastic version of the piece in Book 3, one that should only be played by an advanced student. Not even Hollywood was exempt from the fad:

> [It] even inspired the campy 1946 Hollywood film hit *Humoresque*, starring John Garfield as an aspiring concert violinist (dubbed by Isaac Stern), Joan Crawford as his neurotic benefactress, and the irrepressible Oscar Levant (sample dialogue: ''Martinis are an acquired taste, like Ravel'').[269]

Though Humoresque has lost some of its old notoriety as a pop favorite, it tends to be one of the more easily recognizable tunes in the Suzuki repertoire.

JEAN BECKER
11 May 1833 – 10 October 1884
Gavotte
Era: Romantic

Like so many of the composers who wrote pieces in the Suzuki books, Jean Becker's first teacher was his father. Later he studied with Aloys Kettenus, from whom Becker eventually took the position of head of Mannheim's Nationaltheater orchestra.[270] In the 1860s Becker successfully toured throughout Europe, where he became known as the "German Paganini."[271] His playing style incorporated German and French styles: a combination of seriousness and brilliance.[272]

---

269 Lipscomb 101
270 Mill 49
271 Mill 49
272 Bachmann 342

One of Becker's particular interests was the string quartet. He played with various groups, once even with Clara Schumann (wife of Robert Schumann). Becker's most illustrious string quartet was the Quartetto Fiorentino, a group which

> devoted itself exclusively to quartet playing. It was recognized as the outstanding quartet of its time, setting standards of ensemble, musicianship and repertory that signaled the beginning of professional quartet playing; equally important was its role in developing audiences for chamber music and inspiring interest in amateur quartet playing.[273]

JOHANN SEBASTIAN BACH
21 March 1685 – 28 July 1750
Gavotte in D Major
Era: Baroque, 1731
Genre: Baroque Dance Suite

Gavotte in D Major is from the Orchestra Suite No. 3 in D Major, BWV 1068. It was written when Bach was 46 years old, when he was living in Leipzig. Two years prior to writing this piece Bach had become the director of the Collegium Musicum, a group devoted to instrumental music.[274] The Collegium Musicum was a leisure-time activity for him. His real job was as music director and cantor at the Thomasschule, where he was required to write choral music. By 1729, though, Bach had already written enough choral music to last the rest of his life, so he had the time to look elsewhere for inspiration. Bach was notoriously unwilling to bow to authority, so he must have enjoyed working with a group of musicians who allowed him the freedom to compose what he wished.

If there is anything that calls the date of this composition into question it was Bach's tendency to revive Cöthen works for the use of Collegium Musicum. Thus there may be a slight chance that the

---

273 Mill 49
274 Seaton 322

Gavotte in D Major was written between 1717 and 1723.[275] For more biographical information on Johann Sebastian Bach see page 11.

JOHANN SEBASTIAN BACH
21 March 1685 – 28 July 1750
Bourrée
Era: Baroque, written around 1720
Genre: suite for solo cello

Bach wrote the Bourrée during his time as Kapellmeister in Cöthen. It is from BWV 1009, the Suite for Cello no. 3, 5th movement. His previous employment at Weimar had been terminated violently when he broke his contract with the prince and was imprisoned for almost a month. Bach's relations with his employers had always been tenuous up to that point (he was a man who didn't suffer fools, and he rarely ran into anyone that he didn't consider foolish). It must have been a relief, then, to work for Prince Leopold of Anhalt-Cöthen, a man who was a good musician in his own right and who believed in keeping an excellent orchestra. While working for Prince Leopold, Bach returned from a trip to find his wife Maria Barbara dead and already buried.[276] That same year, 1720, the cello suites were written. It is difficult to imagine that his personal tragedy failed to influence his works during this time. By the end of 1721 he married a professional musician named Anna Magdalena Wilken, a woman sixteen years younger than he was. That same year Prince Leopold married a woman who was both uninterested in music and desirous of turning her husband away from pursuing it.[277] Bach started searching for a new job.

Much of Bach's instrumental music, including the famous *Brandenburg* Concertos and violin sonatas and partitas, were written during his time in Cöthen. Interestingly, the *Brandenburg* Concertos, some of the most popular music for chamber ensemble ever composed, were written as a job application to the Marquess of Brandenburg: an

---

275 Seaton 323
276 Seaton 172
277 Seaton 318

application that was ultimately unsuccessful.[278] Bach did manage to leave Anhalt-Cöthen in 1723. He was the third choice for the Kantor position in Leipzig, a post that he was only able to acquire because Telemann and Grapner turned it down.[279] Prince Leopold, unlike his employer in Weimar, sent him off with his blessing and excellent recommendations.

For a more biographical information on Johann Sebastian Bach see page 11.

BOURRÉE

Bach's Bourrée comes from the Cello Suite no. III, BWV 1009. Because it was written for cello, the piece was originally in the keys of C major and minor (in the Suzuki violin book it is in the keys of G major and minor). The Cello Suites are organized into a group of six dance suites. They are among the first literature written specifically for the cello (the viola de gamba had been the continuo instrument of choice previously, and would soon fall out of use).[280] There are several pieces in the Suzuki literature from the Cello Suites, pieces that work admirably well for the violin, though cellists may argue that these arrangements cannot compare to the original.

A bourrée is a dance that originated in Auvergne, France, and in its earliest form involved young men flapping their arms around. When the dance moved to the French court it became more refined.[281] It can be either in a 2/4 or 2/2 meter and should be played *allegro molto*. Other names for a "bourrée" include borry, borea, boree and burre.[282]

---

278 Boyd 68
279 Seaton 319
280 De Place
281 Winold 70
282 Pedigo 2

CHAPTER 4: SUZUKI BOOK 4

FRIEDRICH (FRITZ) SEITZ
12 June 1848 – 22 May 1918
Concerto No. 2, 3rd Movement
Concerto No. 5, 1st Movement
Concerto No. 5, 3rd Movement
Era: Romantic to Modern (Concerto no. 2 published 1912)
Genre: Pupil's Concerto

Fritz Seitz is the most contemporary of the composers in the Suzuki books (with the exception of Shinichi Suzuki), and the only one whose writing can be considered a part of the modern time period. His included works are, however, meant as preparation for the great Classical and Romantic concertos and hardly representative of any of the turbulent musical styles of the twentieth century.

Seitz was a German composer, violinist and teacher. He grew up on a farm near Gotha. At age seventeen he joined the Gotha regiment and by eighteen had fought in the Seven Weeks' War.[283] After the war he studied violin with Karl Wilhelm Uhlrich and John Christoph Lauterbach.[284] From 1869 – 1808 Seitz worked jobs in various orchestras in Sonderhausen, Magdeburg, Dessau and Bayreuth, where in 1888 he was the concertmaster of the Wagner Festival.[285] During this time he also became famous as a touring soloist throughout Europe.

---

283 Rivers
284 Rivers
285 Rivers

Seitz wrote many instructional pieces for the violin. This number includes eight pupil's concertos; three violin, cello and piano trios; and several other character pieces.[286] Within his *Kleine Violinschule* are the pieces we learn in the Suzuki books. Concerto no. 2 was published in 1912 in Magdeburg, close to the end of his life.[287] His most famous student, Marlene Dietrich, would eventually become a film star. As a young woman she wanted to become a concert violinist and was reputed to be a very good player.[288]

ANTONIO VIVALDI
4 March 1678 – 28 July 1741
Concerto in A Minor, 1ˢᵗ and 3ʳᵈ movements
Era: Baroque, published 1711
Genre: Baroque concerto

If any music seems to capture the color, fullness, and excitement
of Venetian life, it is Vivaldi's concertos. – Heller 66

Antonio Vivaldi, nicknamed the "red priest" for the color of his hair, was a veritable superstar of the Baroque era. He was a trained violinist, as was his father (Giovanni Battista Vivaldi played for St. Mark's cathedral in Venice).[289] Vivaldi took orders as a priest in 1703. Due to an unfortunate chest condition he lost his voice during mass very soon after his ordination, which was why, he explained later, he

---

286 Rivers
287 Jameson
288 Rivers
289 Loft 65

did not celebrate the mass for the next twenty-five years.[290] (E. van der Straeten has a different theory on Vivaldi's fall from grace: he suddenly had a musical idea in the middle of celebrating Mass, left the altar, wrote it down in the vestry, and then came back to finish the Mass, thereby ensuring his suspension from officiating.[291]) It is possible that Vivaldi never intended to make the priesthood his sole career, and certainly during his time there were so many priests in Venice it must have been necessary for most of them to earn an income outside the church. In August of 1703 Vivaldi started his first job as combined priest and violin instructor at the Ospedale della Pietà, an orphanage.[292]

This was no ordinary orphanage: the Conservatory of the Hospital of the Pietà in Venice took in girls and gave many of them extensive musical educations.[293] There were many of these "hospital" orphanages in Venice (so called because they were attached to hospitals), and four of them in particular acquired the reputation of conservatories.[294] The hospital orchestras were so popular and such a novelty that people came from all over Europe to see their performances. Many of the girls attained a high level of virtuosity on their instruments before the age of 12 or 13, when they would typically leave to be married.

Vivaldi taught, composed and acquired instruments for the Pietà, as well as sporadically celebrating mass.[295] His compositions were made famous by the Pietà girls. Vivaldi's concertos were also played widely throughout Europe, and in particular his use of ritornello form was very influential to other composers. J.S. Bach, for example, was fascinated by Vivaldi's concertos and transcribed many of them for the harpsichord or organ.[296] The form of the Baroque Venetian concerto was emulated all over Northern Europe, eventually evolving into the Classical concerto.[297]

After 1709 Vivaldi alternated between touring and working in Venice (periodically at the Pietà, periodically for other patrons). He was in high demand as a teacher, a composer and a performer. Philipp

---

290 Heller 43
291 Straeten 156
292 Heller 43
293 Loft 65
294 Heller 28
295 Randel 953
296 Straeten 157
297 White 5

of Hesse-Darmstadt, governor of Mantua, employed Vivaldi as his court composer between 1718 and 1720.[298] In the 1720s Vivaldi was Kapellmeister to the Bohemian Count Morzin.[299] By the end of his life, though, his popularity had declined. In 1741 he decided to move to Vienna in an attempt to regain some of his previous fame.[300] Only a month after his arrival he died and was buried in a pauper's grave.

Vivaldi was forgotten for many years after his death. His music was only unburied after Mendelssohn revived Bach's *Saint Matthew Passion* in 1829. During the subsequent rage for Baroque music Vivaldi's concertos were rediscovered and have been popular ever since.[301]

CONCERTO IN A MINOR, OPUS 3, NO. 6, RV 356

During his lifetime Vivaldi was one of three major Venetian composers (the other two were Tommaso Albinoni and Benedetto Marcello). The Venetians tended to write concertos with three long movements, a trend that would catch on throughout Europe and lead to conventional three-movement Classical and Romantic concertos.[302] Venetian concertos, as exemplified by the Concerto in A Minor, are generally comprised of two faster movements with memorable themes surrounding an almost operatic slow movement.[303] (The slow movement of this concerto is in Book 5.) Vivaldi must have preferred to write for the violin as he wrote at least 240 violin concertos, roughly a third of his enormous concerto output.[304] He once boasted that he could "compose a concerto in all its parts more quickly than a copyist can write them down."[305]

This particular concerto was a part of a collection published in 1711 titled *L'estro armonico* Op. 3 ("harmonic inspiration" or "harmonic

---

298 Heller 137
299 Heller 148
300 Randel 953
301 Loft 66
302 Hutchings 134
303 Hutchings 135
304 Foures 3
305 Foures 3

fire"[306]), and was dedicated to the Grand Prince Fernando of Tuscany.[307] Vivaldi had, at the time, just been rehired at the Pietà. (He had been laid off in 1709, probably through no negligence of his duties but for reasons of economy and because he had trained his students so well they were able to replace him as teachers.[308]) *L'estro armonico* was the first of Vivaldi's works to be published outside of Italy, by Etienne Roger in Amsterdam. This change reflected both the superiority of the engraving process used in Amsterdam and the growing popularity of Italian music in Northern Europe, particularly Germany.[309]

Opus 3 was a set of twelve concertos written over the course of many years. The oldest piece in the opus is clearly a concerto grosso in the style of Archangelo Corelli. Concerto in A Minor no. 6 is one of the most evolved of the opus, already taking the mature form of a three movement Baroque concerto.[310]

One of the key thematic devices that Vivaldi uses is ritornello form, which is especially evident in the first movement of the Concerto in A Minor. A ritornello is a sort of refrain that is restated throughout a piece, sometimes in different keys or octaves or entirely disguised as a variation. Usually the ritornello is played by the tutti, (full orchestra). Ritornello alternates with the "soloist" part, which is often more virtuosic.[311] (It was common practice during the Baroque era for soloists to play all tutti sections with the rest of the orchestra.) These themes were often meant to sound improvised, though many of them were in fact written down.[312] One of Vivaldi's defining characteristics is his tendency to repeat the opening motive of the ritornello in the solo part.[313] The root of ritornello is found in opera: its original definition was the instrumental interlude between verses of a song.[314]

---

306 Heller 57
307 Talbot 818
308 Talbot 817-18
309 Talbot 818
310 Heller 61
311 White 5
312 Hutchings 134
313 White 6
314 Claudio Montiverdi's operas, for example *Orfeo*, offer an idea of what ritornello sounded like in its original form. The device is simple but extremely effective, especially in some of the faster tempos.

In many ways Vivaldi's concertos sound Romantic, if by "Romantic" we mean impassioned, expressive and brilliant.[315] They are deceptively simple. Though not as difficult to play as a Paganini caprice, a really good performance of a Vivaldi concerto requires a great deal of musical sensitivity. Probably Vivaldi wanted violinists to incorporate crescendo and decrescendo in his concertos, despite the popular belief that these dynamics weren't widespread until the Mannheim school of the Classical era.[316] The violin was, after all, believed to have the same ability to express complex emotion as the human voice. Finally, it is important to remember that Vivaldi himself thought of the concerto genre as one which was "an expression of spontaneous inspiration, playfulness, challenge and sheer pleasure in the music."[317]

The first and third movements of the Concerto in A Minor have been edited in the Suzuki books by Tivadar Nachez, a student of the nineteenth century violin virtuoso Joseph Joachim.[318] Because of Nachez's additions, the notes in the Suzuki versions of the Vivaldi concertos may be different from other editions. Editing of some sort is important for authentic realizations of Baroque concertos which, as originally published, were really only meant to be frameworks for improvisation. Vivaldi would have expected his music to be ornamented and changed by each individual performer, not played exactly as written.[319] An interesting study for the advanced violinist would be to take a copy of the 1711 manuscript, study it, and then make his or her own decisions for embellishments. As the Concerto in A Minor stands in the Suzuki books, however, the changes are often astoundingly beautiful and well worth learning. One example of these embellishments is the arpeggios in the middle of the third movement, inspired by Vivaldi's musical line but actually an invention of Nachez.

---

315 Hutchings 141
316 Hutchings 142
317 Foures 3
318 Wartberg
319 Wartberg

JOHANN SEBASTIAN BACH
21 March 1685 – 28 July 1750
Concerto for Two Violins, Vivace
Era: Baroque, written between 1717 and 1750
Genre: Baroque Concerto

Bach's Concerto for Two Violin and Orchestra in D minor may have been written in Cöthen during his time as Kapellmeister for Prince Leopold of Saxe-Anhalt or when he was a member of the Collegium Musicum in Leipzig. Some authorities believe that most of Bach's instrumental music was written in Cöthen because of Prince Leopold's interest in music.[320] While it is true that his job in Leipzig required him for the most part to compose organ and vocal music for the church (while there he wrote five complete cycles of cantatas for the church year, a staggering 300 cantatas altogether), as a part of Leipzig's Collegium Musicum he would also have been required to write instrumental music. Between 1729 and 1749 Bach participated in Leipzig's Collegium Musicum (a group of musicians who gathered to put on public concerts).[321] The three surviving violin concertos could just as easily have been written during these twenty years.

Luckily the Concerto for Two Violins and the Concerto in A minor in Book 7 were willed to Bach's son Carl Philip Emanuel instead of his oldest son Wilhelm Friedemann.[322] Wilhelm Friedemann seemed to have little interest in preserving his father's legacy, so much of our knowledge of J.S. Bach comes from the pieces that were given to other sons.[323] These pieces in particular play a pivotal role in the Suzuki repertoire, preparing students for the classical concertos of Mozart while giving them a taste of some of the more complex literature of the Baroque era.

For more biographical information on Johann Sebastian Bach see page 11.

---

320 Lyons
321 Seaton 343
322 Kilian intro
323 One very interesting part of the Notebook for Willhelm Friederich Bach: it contains a reference of how J.S. Bach expected ornaments to be executed.

THE CONCERTO FOR TWO VIOLINS IN D MINOR, BWV 1043

The Concerto for Two Violins is Italianate in structure, with two quick movements around a slow, pensive one.[324] Its fugal exposition has a four-bar subject that provides the pillars around which the three solo sections are built.[325] This piece is usually the student's first encounter with the unbelievable intricacy of many of Bach's compositions. Bach, unlike most composers of his time, did not, as a rule, want performers to improvise on his music. He provided all of the ornamentation himself. As such, it is sometimes difficult to figure out exactly what the melody is, which notes are just ornamentation, and where the phrases begin and end.

The two movements that are not included in the Suzuki books are both exceptionally fun to play and are excellent additional repertoire.

324 Lyons
325 Boyd 493

CHAPTER 5: SUZUKI BOOK 5

JOHANN SEBASTIAN BACH
21 March 1685 – 28 July 1750
Gavotte
Era: Baroque, written in 1720
Genre: Baroque Dance Suite

Gavotte is yet another movement from Bach's Suite for Unaccompanied Cello, in particular Suite VI, BWV 1012. This gavotte, in its original form, has a variety of double stops that may prove interesting to the more advanced student. The more advanced student may, however, not be so much interested in filling out the missing notes in the cello repertoire as starting to learn the *Sonatas and Partitas for Solo Violin*. See page 11 for biographical information about Johann Sebastian Bach. More information about the solo cello suites is on page 51.

ANTONIO VIVALDI
4 March 1678 – 28 July 1741
Concerto in A Minor, 2nd movement
Era: Baroque, publisher 1711
Genre: Baroque concerto

The operatic quality of Vivaldi's concertos is best observed in his second movements. They often begin with a brief tutti[326] introduction followed by the solo for the rest of the piece (usually written in AB or binary form,).[327] These slow movements are the instrumental equivalent of the vocalist's aria, with the same lyricism and opportunity for ornamentation as Baroque Italian opera.[328]

For more biographical information on Antonio Vivaldi and his Concerto in A Minor see page 54.

ANTONIO VIVALDI
4 March 1678 – 28 July 1741
Concerto in G Minor, op 12
Era: Baroque, published in 1729
Genre: Baroque concerto

Between 1723 and 1729 Vivaldi was no longer officially employed as music director at the Pietà, but he had been hired to write the orphanage two concertos a month for a sequim each. He was also required to direct three or four rehearsals each time he came through Venice (at this time Vivaldi was spending most of his time traveling through Italy). This job resulted in over 140 concertos, one of which was the Concerto in G Minor.[329]

This particular concerto in G minor, op. 12 (Vivaldi wrote so many concertos in G minor it boggles the mind), was one of his last concerto publications.[330] He was dissatisfied with the financial returns, and decided from then on to do the "more profitable trade in manuscripts, for which the current price was a guinea per concerto; and indeed no work of his published after op. 12 appeared without his proven consent."[331] The manuscript trade, essentially, involved finding wealthy patrons to

---

326 In the Baroque era, tuttis were played by the soloist as well as the orchestra. Solo sections would then give the soloists a chance to display virtuosic skills with orchestral accompaniment.
327 White 9
328 White 9
329 Talbot 819
330 Talbot 819
331 Talbot 819

buy individual manuscripts of his concertos that he wrote "especially for them."[332]

The style of the Concerto in G Minor, op 12 is very different from the Concerto in A Minor, leading many to think that it was not written by Vivaldi. It is, however, more likely that Vivaldi gradually moved on to a more Classical style in the nearly twenty years between publications.

For more information on Antonio Vivaldi see page 54.

CARL MARIA VON WEBER
18 November 1786 – 5 June 1826
Country Dance
Era: Romantic

For a biography of Carl Maria von Weber see page 23.

KARL DITTERS VON DITTERSDORF
2 November 1739 – 24 October 1799
German Dance
Era: Classical

Karl Ditters was born a commoner, the son of the imperial costumier at the Austrian royal court. He was educated in a Jesuit school and given violin lessons from the time he was seven years old.[333] At eleven Karl was accepted into his first orchestra, and as a teenager he gained enough of a reputation as a composer to receive commissions for concertos and symphonies.[334] He worked for Prince Joseph Friedrich von Sachsen-Hildburghausen until he turned 22.

Ditters' professional life from his early twenties until his death was dependent on a succession of aristocratic patrons. After 1769 he worked on and off for Prince-Bishop Count Philipp Gotthard von Schaffgotsch

---

332 Heller 56
333 Grave 386
334 Grave 386

in Johannisberg.[335] Due to financial difficulties Schaffgotsch rehired Ditters in various non-musical capacities, both as an official in the town of Freiwaldau (a post which required his ennoblement, hence the new name "Karl Ditters von Dittersdorf"), and as his head forester.[336] It seems doubtful that the composer was particularly skilled at either job. He was, however, well known and liked as a musician.

The authenticity of much of the work attributed to Dittersdorf is questionable. Like George Frideric Handel, Dittersdorf was so famous in his day that others published works in his name in order to sell more copies. Margaret Grave writes that "[his] works span nearly the entire development of the Viennese Classical Style and include substantial contributions to most of the popular genres of his day."[337] These genres include symphonies, concertos, chamber music, church music and opera.[338]

FRANCESCO MARIA VERACINI
1 February 1690 – 31 October 1768
Gigue from Sonata in D Minor, (opus 1, no. 5)
Era: Baroque, first published in 1744.
Genre: Baroque sonata

Francesco Maria Veracini was born in Florence to a family of musicians. His first violin teacher was his uncle, Antonio. In 1699 he moved to Rome, where he studied with G. A. Bernabei and Francesco Gasparini.[339] Much of his youthful career as a performer is undocumented, and the first evidence of a permanent position is as first violinist at St. Mark's Venice in 1713.[340] It was around that time that Veracini played for the illustrious violinist Giuseppe Tartini, impressing him so much that Tartini went into retirement for a year to improve his bow arm.[341] Veracini worked in London for two years before returning and

---

335 Grave 387
336 Grave 387
337 Grave 387
338 Grave 387
339 Loft 151
340 Straeten 166
341 Winn forward

soon thereafter was invited to Dresden, where he became a part of the musical court at age 27.[342]

While in Dresden Veracini became embroiled in a rivalry between the Italian and native German musicians. It is possible that his higher pay grade was partially responsible, as was his notorious ego. The conflict was led by the court's concertmaster, Johann Georg Pisendel. (Also included among the German players in the court was Christian Pezold, the man who wrote Minuet 3 and possibly Minuet 2 in Book 1.[343]) Conflict would soon lead to tragedy:

> The . . . story has it that Veracini was asked to perform, at sight, a Pisendel concerto in the presence of the court. Pisendel, however, had already secretly coached one of the back-stand orchestral members in the same work. Immediately after Veracini's effort, the other violinist performed the concerto, to the approbation of the court and to the intense annoyance of the Italian virtuoso. In any event, Veracini took the extraordinary measure of leaping (in 1722) from a third-floor window, with resulting hip and leg fractures that left him lame for life.[344]

This unfortunate incident sheds light on Veracini's unique personality. His contemporaries considered him to be insane, eccentric and arrogant.[345] He was also regarded as one of Europe's finest violinists.[346] In many ways he is the ultimate stereotype of a career artist.

After his sojourn in Dresden Veracini traveled around Europe, performing in Italy, Prague and London. He wrote a great deal of church music as well as opera (for a few seasons, in fact, he wrote and conducted for the opera house that rivaled Handel's[347]). In 1745 he moved back to Italy. During the journey home he was shipwrecked and lost all of his belongings, including his two Steiner violins (which he had named Peter and Paul).[348] For the remainder of his life he per-

---

342 Loft 151
343 Hill 420
344 Loft 151-2
345 Hill 421
346 Hill 420
347 Hill 420
348 Straeten 167

formed less and less.[349] In Veracini's last years he served as a church musician in Florence, taking the posts of maestro di cappella for the Vallambrosan fathers from 1755 until his death and a similar post for the Theatine fathers from 1758 on.[350]

As a composer Veracini seems almost modern, "especially in his thematic material, its bold harmonic treatment, and the characteristic chromatic passages."[351] He was misunderstood, perhaps, by his contemporaries, who thought that his works were "capricious and bizarre."[352] Part of his negative reception as a composer could have been his arrogance and overwhelming egotism, not uncommon among virtuosos of every day and age.

GIGUE FROM SONATA IN D MINOR (OPUS 2, NO. 7)

Though Veracini wrote many vocal works for church and opera, he is best remembered for his violin sonatas.[353] Opus 2, a collection of twelve sonatas, was published in 1744 and dedicated to the Elector of Saxony, who was also King August III of Poland.[354] The dedication is surprising, considering that he had left the Elector's service twenty years prior to publishing these sonatas and was living in England and Italy at the time.[355] The pieces were published in London and Florence simultaneously. It is possible that Veracini was trying to regain his former position in Dresden, and, if so, he failed in his attempt.[356] Veracini titled his work *Sonata accademica für Violine und Klavier,*"or "Academic sonatas for the violin and keyboard." The title "academic" indicates that he meant for it to be played by and for professional musicians rather than amateurs.[357]

---

349 Loft 153
350 Hill 421
351 Straeten 168
352 Straeten 168
353 Loft 153
354 Loft 153
355 Kolneder
356 Kolneder
357 Kolneder

These pieces don't have the same maturity in form as sonatas by Handel and Bach, and are in style more like suites.[358] (At the time the same type of music was called a partita in Germany, a suite in England and a sonata in Italy,[359] hence the name "sonata" by an Italian composer.) Musicians at the time were expected to infuse their own personalities and ornamentation into their performances rather than sticking to one authoritative version.[360] In theory, then, this is a piece that the advanced student could embellish to suit her own preferences.

The origins of the Gigue are, as its name implies, in dance; in particular, rope-dancing.[361] (Other names for the gigue dance form are jig and giga.[362]) E.L. Winn suggests that, when playing this particular Gigue:

> There is a tendency to play the giga too rapidly. It is lively but not fast, as allegro, at the time, was not especially rapid. Even in dance forms there was dignity. One must be very careful to keep the bow at an easy angle on the strings; that is, string transfers must be made easily, with the arm and wrist very flexible. The spiccato in the middle and the lower half of the bow is useful. Contrasts between the staccato and legato must be observed. [363]

Gigues were some of the most popular of the Baroque dances, and, like most Baroque dances, were divided into two parts: one in the tonic key and the other in the dominant key. Veracini's Gigue starts in G and then after the repeat switches to the key of D.

---

358 Winn 1
359 Winn 1
360 Adas *The Eighteenth Century Continuo Sonata, Volume II.* viii
361 Winn 1
362 Pedigo 3
363 Winn 1

CHAPTER 6: SUZUKI BOOK 6

ARCHANGELO CORELLI
17 February 1653 – 8 January 1713
La Folia
Era: Baroque, written around 1700
Genre: sonata for violin and keyboard

Archangelo Corelli grew up in a family of some affluence in Fusignano, Italy. Like J.S. Bach he was the youngest son and he, too, lost his father early in life and was sent to live with relatives.[364] His first lessons were from local teachers, but by 1666 he had moved to Bologna, where he took violin lessons from Giovanni Benvenuti and Leonardo Brugnoli.[365] (Corelli considered himself a part of the

---

364 Corelli never actually knew his father as he died six days before his son's birth. Straeten 137
365 Talbot 457

Bolognese school, a tradition that was also associated with Martini and was considered one of the best of its day.[366]) In 1671 he moved to Rome, where he was soon one of its foremost violinists. He had a reputation for becoming very physically involved in his music, contorting his face and moving around excessively.[367] Corelli also taught violin, and was particularly strict. Among his more famous students were Geminiani and Locatelli.[368]

Corelli worked for the Elector of Bavaria from 1679 to 1681. Most of the rest of his life was spent in Italy, in particular Rome:[369] in 1681 he entered the service of Queen Christina of Sweden (who, despite her title, lived in Rome) and would later change his patron to Cardinal Pamphili.[370] In 1690 Corelli went to live at the palace of Cardinal Pietro Ottoboni, where he wrote several sets of chamber music.[371] Ottoboni's establishment included a large-scale orchestra, which Corelli conducted with almost as much acclaim as he had acquired as a violinist.[372] By 1706 Corelli was admitted to the Arcadian Academy in Rome, "receiving the name of Arcomelo Erimanteo."[373] During his lifetime Corelli was known as a modest and mild man.[374] He was also obsessed with saving money. Handel once noted that "he always walked wherever he had to go, and made the most ludicrous excuses whenever we tried to persuade him to take a carriage."[375]

Corelli essentially wrote three different genres of music: the solo sonata, the trio sonata and the concerto. He was considered one of the originators of the concerto, because he was one who helped to make the concerto grosso a distinctive genre.[376] His work in many ways is

---

366 Hutchings 65-6 and 73
367 Loft 49
368 Loft 49
369 Straeten 138
370 Talbot 458
371 Talbot 458
372 Straeten 139
373 Talbot 458
374 Talbot 457
375 Straeten 143. And, yes, this example proves that famous composers were capable of being prudent with their finances.
376 Hutchings 31

a synthesis of the best in music of his predecessors, both in the art of playing the violin and of the sonata form.[377] Corelli preferred to write music that required beautiful tone and expression rather than virtuoso display.[378] (In direct contrast to composers like Veracini, who were far more interested in showing off.)

During a time when most music was written, performed a few times, and then forgotten, Corelli wrote music that became "classics." That is, many of his pieces were played and performed long after they were no longer the new.[379] He was one of the first composers to become famous for publishing instrumental rather than vocal works.[380] One other interesting fact is that Corelli was "probably the first sonata composer to abandon modality entirely."[381]

La Folia

La Folia is the last piece in Corelli's *Opera Quinta, Parte Seconda* (from a book dedicated to *sonate de camera*). The *Opera Quinta* was one of Corelli's most successful compositions, serving as a sort of school book for string players.[382] Though it is uncertain when he wrote it, the book was dedicated on Jan 1, 1700 to Sophia Charlotte, Princess of Hanover.[383]

One of the most interesting things about the *Opera Quinta* as a whole is that Corelli wrote his own embellishments in the adagios. In the Baroque era most music (especially slower music) was expected to be performed with embellishments such as trills and turns. These ornaments were hardly ever written into the music. Rather, they were left up to the imagination and were considered an essential improvisational skill for the accomplished performer. It is difficult for modern

---

377 Straeten 140
378 Straeten 140
379 Talbot 457
380 Hutchings 31
381 Pedigo 9. "Modality" was the theoretical system behind composition used before tonality. With the tonal era came the major and minor scale systems rather than the church modes, scales based on a different succession of whole and half steps.
382 Chrysander, forward to Complete Works of Archangelo Corelli, Book III op. 5
383 Chrysander, forward to Complete Works of Archangelo Corelli, Book III op. 5

violinists, most of whom have not been trained to improvise, to figure out what these ornaments should be. The *Opera Quinta*, then, serves as an excellent pedagogical tool for learning what a professional violinist would have done in the day of Corelli.

A "folia" or "follia" is a type of fourteenth century Portuguese dance. It has been used as the basis for theme-and-variation type songs by composers of many eras.[384] The version in the Suzuki books is in some ways different from the 23-variation original (some of the variations are slightly different, some have been left out). Abraham Loft indicates that the piece was written to be pedagogical, and that "those desiring an orderly exploration of Corellian technique . . . as an introduction to the sonatas rather than as a culmination thereof, will profit from study of the *Follia* variations."[385] La Folia, then, should be a good preparation for many of the techniques used in Baroque violin music.

It may also be instructive for students to listen to various recordings of La Folia, as the piano part in the Suzuki accompaniment book is pretty but not particularly representative of Corelli's true style.

GEORGE FRIDERIC HANDEL
23 February 1685 – 14 April 1759
Sonata no. 3
(also known as Sonata No. 12 in F major, opus 1)
Era: Baroque, written between 1724 and 1726
Genre: Violin sonata

Though Handel's great fame comes primarily from Italian opera and English oratorio, "in fact he contributed to every musical genre current in his time, both vocal and instrumental."[386] Included among these are about fifty pieces of chamber music, six of which were violin and keyboard sonatas.[387] For more biographical information about Handel see page 19.

---

384 Loft 63
385 Loft 63
386 Hicks 747
387 Loft 98

SONATA NO. 3

Handel's first sonatas for violin and continuo were written between 1724 and 1726. Possibly they were written for Princesses Anne and Caroline of England, for whom Handel was music-master.[388]

These sonatas were given the opus number "one" by its second publisher, a number which means nothing in its usual chronological sense as Handel was around 40 at the time and had been producing works of music prolifically for years. The first date of publication for these sonatas was recorded as 1722, when Jeanne Roger in Amsterdam supposedly brought out "Sonatas for Flute, Violin or Oboe, with Basso Continuo, by G. F. Handel"[389] There were twelve works in the set, three of which were for the violin; originally they were listed as Opus 1, number 3, in A; Opus 1, number 14, in A; and Opus 1, number 15, in E flat. The legitimacy of this publication date is, however, suspicious for several reasons: the violin sonatas had not yet been written, and Jeanne Roger died in 1722.[390] Whoever had published the works had used plates that had been engraved by the London publisher John Walsh, the elder, who had been Handel's principal publisher in England since 1711.

The first edition had probably been pirated; it had many mistakes and omissions when compared to the manuscripts. Walsh did bring out his own edition around 1732, under the title *Solos for a German Flute, a Hoboy or Violin with a Thorough Bass for the Harpsichord or Bass Violin Compos'd by Mr. Handel.*[391] Walsh noted that "This is more Corect than the former Edition,"[392] possibly the result of substituting two sonatas instead of nos. 14 and 15. Instead, he put in numbers 10 (in G minor) and 12 (in F major, or Sonata no. 3 as it is called in the Suzuki books). Number 13 in D (Sonata no. 4 in the Suzuki books) was still not included. This last one was published by Chrysander in the Händel-Gesellschaft edition in the late 19th century.[393] The sev-

---

388 Best XIII
389 Loft 98
390 Best XIII
391 Loft 98-9
392 Loft 99
393 Loft 99

enth sonata, which was marked in one of the early editions as an oboe sonata, was later discovered to have been intended for the violin by Handel himself.[394] This one is labeled Opus 1, no. 6 in G minor. Two other sonatas are thought to have been originally written for the violin, HWV 359 for the flute and HWV 358.[395]

Part of the problem with these sonatas was that it was clear from their first publications that several had *not* been written by Handel. The 1722 first editions of sonatas number 14 and 15, not included in the Suzuki books, had the note: "This is not Mr. Handel's" written on them by an early commentator.[396] The 1733 reprint, which contains the replacements for 14 and 15 (numbers 10 and 12, which is Sonata no. 3), has a similar written comment: "Not Mr. Handel's solo."[397] In other words, this first Handel sonata that the Suzuki student learns wasn't written by Handel at all. Whoever wrote it, this sonata is a good pedagogical tool and, moreover, is just fun to play.

Abraham Loft's comments on Sonata no. 3 in F major are that the dotted figures in the final Allegro must be played as triplets. Turning dotted figures into triplets was a common practice in the Baroque era, in this case made even more necessary in order to match the rhythm of the continuo.[398]

OTHER WORKS OF INTEREST FOR PLAYING AND LISTENING:

All but the last two of Handel's violin sonatas (including four which were definitely written by someone else) can be found in the Henle Urtext edition: *Seven Sonatas for Violin and Figured Bass*, arranged by Rohring. This edition includes a part for cello, which is not so much necessary for an effective execution of the piece as a bonus for the young violinist who would like to learn to play with more than just a keyboard. Handel also wrote a number of sonatas for two violins and cello (basso continuo) that would make interesting chamber music for the young Handel enthusiast.

---

394 Best XIII
395 Best XV
396 Loft 99
397 Loft 99
398 Loft 107

JOSEPH HECTOR FIOCCO
20 Jan 1703 – 21 June 1741
Allegro
Era: Baroque

Joseph Hector Fiocco was a Belgian composer, organist and harpsichordist. He was employed at various times during his short life as a choirmaster, musician in a ducal court, and music director in various areas in and around Brussels.[399] After his death his wife sold all of his compositions to the collegiate church of St. Michel and St. Gudule.[400] Most of his larger works, for the most part composed for the church, have slipped into obscurity.[401] His music incorporates French and Italian styles and was strongly influenced by Couperin.[402]

Allegro's origins are dubious, but it probably comes from one of his harpsichord pieces.[403] (Fiocco was known during his lifetime for his harpsichord skills.) It is often played as an encore.

JEAN-PHILIPPE RAMEAU
25 September 1683 – 12 September 1764
Gavotte
Era: Classical

---

399 Baratz 880
400 Baratz 880
401 Elie
402 Baratz 880
403 Elie

Jean-Philippe Rameau was the first composer to achieve fame in the field of French opera after the death of Jean-Baptiste Lully. He was born in Dijon, France, the son of the organist of the cathedral.[404] After a Jesuit education and music studies, Rameau followed his father's footsteps and at age nineteen had his first post as organist at Clermont-Ferrand.[405]

Twenty years later he had published two books on music theory, a passion of his since his childhood. By his late forties Rameau was hired as music master of the household of la Poupeliniere,[406] and under the influence of his new employer and the encouragement of Voltaire he wrote his first opera at the age of fifty.[407] Though this first attempt was a failure, it marked the beginning of Rameau's very successful career as an opera composer. He was derided by several factions, first by promoters of Lully's work and then by the new rage for Italian comic opera (sparked by the opera *La Serva Padrona*, by Pergolesi[408]). The conflict between French and Italian opera actually went so far as to acquire a nickname, "*la guerre des bouffons*," or the war of the buffoons.[409] Nonetheless Rameau was very popular during his lifetime and was eventually even hired as composer of chamber music at the French court.[410]

Among Rameau's most popular operas are *Castor et Pollux* (1737), *Les Indes galantes* (1735) and *Dardanus* (1737).[411]

GEORGE FRIDERIC HANDEL
23 February 1685 – 4 April 1759
Sonata no. 4
(also known as Sonata no. 13 in D major, Opus 1)
Era: Baroque, written between 1749 and 1751
Genre: Baroque violin sonata

---

404 Ewen 152
405 Eewen 152
406 The Poupeliniere orchestra's next music master was Gossec, writer of the Gavotte at the end of Book 1!
407 Ewen 152
408 Ewen 151
409 Ewen 152
410 Ewen 152
411 Ewen 152

Sonata no. 4 in D major (HWV 371) was not a part of Handel's original Opus 1. It was probably written between 1749 and 1751, making it one of Handel's last instrumental works.[412] It is one of his most emotionally compelling pieces of chamber music for violin.

The first movement of Sonata no. 4, marked affettuoso (affectionate), involves constant clashes between the violin and the bass. There are several intervals of 9^{ths}. The first four notes, in fact, "prove nettlesome, rather than affectionate: D-F#-A-E! The E is not only foreign, but also long, insistent, stubborn, and for the moment, unresolved."[413] This unlikely beginning is followed by tension throughout the movement. Abraham Loft suggests that:

> For the performer, the problem is two-edged: either he plays the movement with bland impartiality, plodding through all the notes, sweet and otherwise, unaware of their varying potency, or else, recognizing the acerb nature of the sustained "foreign" tones, he lays into them with relentless pressure, so that the emphasis becomes leaden and unappetizing. Rather, the sustained irritant notes must be played with easy stroke, with warm but not sizzling vibrato, so that the note resonates, glows, lending its particular intensity to the otherwise normal progressions of the music in a graceful manner. The shock value of the sounds in this Affettuoso, then, will have that mixture of warmth and hostility that, we are told, so often colors the course of affection, and that certainly seems to be the blend sought by Handel in these lines.[414]

This movement should be analyzed carefully by both student and teacher. It is a piece which almost requires a personal interpretation.

The second movement, Allegro, starts off with a late Baroque device known as the composed acceleration. The rhythm starts with a half note and continues to eighth notes and then sixteenths. One danger with this sort of development, of course, is that of starting out too quickly and crashing upon reaching the sixteenths. Also of note is the "conversa-

---

412 Best XV
413 Loft 100
414 Loft 101

tion" between the bass line and violin (when the violin breaks off, the bass takes over).[415]

The third movement, Largo, has a number of repeating rhythmic figures (for example the first three measures), which can easily become tedious if not arched together into one phrase. Also note that the dotted eighth-sixteenth pairings should either be double-dotted or made into triplets.[416] As with all Baroque slow movements, the performer has the option of adding ornaments such as trills and mordents. There are several texts that explain which embellishments are appropriate, for example C.P.E. Bach's *Essay on the True Art of Playing Keyboard Instruments.*

The final Allegro has an acceleration that is similar to the one in the second movement, but over a longer period of time. There are three separate rhythmic sequences: m. 1-2 (dotted), m. 5-8 (short running) and m. 13-14 (long running). The Suzuki books include the cuts that Handel made to the original score (which was at one time 68 measures long).417

Many of the motifs from Sonata no. 4 either come from earlier works or reappear in later ones: *Solomon*, 1748; the cantata *Da quell giorno fatale*; *Riccardo Primo*, 1727 and Jeptha, 1751.[418] Don't be surprised, then, if you hear echoes of the D major sonata in Handel's other works.

For biographical information on George Frideric Handel see page 19. More information about his sonatas is on page 73.

---

415 Loft 102-3
416 Loft 104
417 Loft 106
418 Best XV

CHAPTER 7: SUZUKI BOOK 7

WOLFGANG AMADEUS MOZART
27 January 1756 – 5 December 1791
Minuet
Era: Classical, written June 1783
Genre: String Quartet

Wolfgang Amadeus Mozart (born Johann Chrisostom Wolfgang Theophilus Mozart) has become famous in recent years, not only for his skill as a musician and composer, but also for his overbearing father: Leopold Mozart. Leopold was what we might call an extreme Suzuki parent, going to the point of composing educational pieces for his children to listen to when they were still in the womb. Wolfgang's father is worthy of note for another reason as well. He was also a musician, a violinist in the court of the Archbishop of Salzburg, and wrote one of the first textbooks on how to play the violin. This book was translated into two languages and used for serious study until several generations after his death. It is still an entertaining read, often amusing and anecdotal, and shows some of the playfulness that would later on become characteristic of his son's compositions.

Mozart the younger, however, was destined for even greater fame. Mention of Wolfgang Amadeus Mozart almost immediately brings to mind a series of age-related accomplishments: his first four violin sonatas were published when he was eight. When he was nine his symphonies were already being performed, and he wrote an opera at fourteen.[419] Leopold toured Wolfgang and his sister Nannerl around Europe as child prodigies, earning his family a great deal of money and fame. When Wolfgang had outgrown his status as child prodigy he was forced to work in Salzburg for the Archbishop, where he "was treated hardly better than a menial servant, subject all the time to personal abuse."[420] Though as a child Wolfgang Mozart's output had been large, none of his early work had excited enough acclaim to establish him elsewhere as an adult. He tried to tour Europe again in his early twenties and ended up back in Salzburg when his venture failed to support itself.

Finally in 1781 the excellent reception of his opera *Idomeneo* convinced him that he could find different employment and he moved to Vienna, where he lived on commissions and teaching.[421] In 1782 he had his first major success in Vienna with the opera *Die Entfuehrung aus dem Serail*, after which he married Constanza Weber. Quite possibly the marriage was brought about through the machinations of her mother (he seemed to prefer her sister), but in his letters he indicated a great deal of affection for his young bride.[422]When he finally did manage to get the position of court composer it was at a reduced salary.[423] (It is safe to say that he was plagued with financial difficulty throughout his life.) In 1791, his last year, Mozart wrote some of his most beautiful and mature music: *The Magic Flute*, *Ave Verum* and the *Requiem*.[424]

---

419 Ewen 215
420 Ewen 215
421 Ewen 215
422 Sadie 286
423 Ewen 216
424 Ewen 216

MINUET

This Minuet comes from Mozart's Quartet in D minor, K 421. It is one of two "Hayden" quartets (K 421 and K 387) and was finished in 1783 in the same month that his new wife Constanze gave birth to their first child.[425] Raimund Leopold, the little boy, only lived for two months.

ARCHANGELO CORELLI
17 February 1653 – 8 January 1713
Courante
Era: Baroque, first published 1712
Genre: Concerto Grosso

Courante is from Corelli's last published opus, which came out in print in December 1712. It is number nine out of a collection of concerti grossi. This one in particular is considered one of the smaller concerti grossi,[426] intended to be played in a little room. Concerto Grosso no. 9 has five movements: Preludio – Allemanda – Corrente – Gavotta – Minuetto. The generally accepted speed for a courante should be around 180-220 per eighth note.[427] A courante (also called corrente or corant allegro) is usually a rapid patter of eighth notes.[428]

The concerto grosso was one of the forerunners of the solo concerto, a mixture of solo and choral elements.[429] A small orchestra of *ripieno* parts would play the tutti sections, and periodically three players (two violinists and a cellist) would come in with solos. Unlike the modern concerto, soloists in a concerto grosso traditionally sit with the rest of the orchestra and play the tutti part whenever they are not required to play their solos. The concerto grosso was recognized as a separate genre, one appropriate for both chamber and church, some-

---

425 Sadie "Mozart" 286
426 Though the English plural of concerto is concertos, the correct plural of concerto grosso is concerti grossi.
427 Pedigo 2
428 Pedigo 2
429 Chrysander preface, Book V Op 6 part II

time at the end of the 17ᵗʰ century.[430] Corelli's concerti grossi were so popular that they were printed and reprinted throughout Europe. They were eventually printed in London around 1730 by Walsh, the same firm that published Handel's sonatas.

For more biographical information on Archangelo Corelli see page 69.

OTHER PIECES FOR STUDENTS

Corelli's concerti grossi are great pieces for students to play, though they do require an entire ensemble if they are to be played in their original form. Possibly a more feasible option for the student who enjoys Corelli would be the *Sonatas da Chiesa a Tre*, which make great chamber music for two violins and piano (or piano and cello). Most of these should be easy enough for the student in Book 7. Bach's *Brandenburg* Concertos are also considered a part of the concerto grosso genre,[431] and are favorites of student violinists.

GEORGE FRIDERIC HANDEL
23 February 1685 – 14 April 1759
Sonata no. 1
(also known as Sonata no.3, in A Major, Opus 1)
Era: Baroque, written about 1724-6
Genre: Violin sonata

Sonata no. 1 was the only piece in the first published set of "Handel" sonatas that can actually be attributed to the composer. This publication, though probably not by Jeanne Roger (who was on the title page), was revised in 1732 by John Walsh into a slightly more legitimate set of 12 sonatas. The new set once again included three sonatas for the violin (as well as sonatas for other instruments), one of which was the sonata found in Book 7. This particular work, then, is the only violin sonata that we can definitively ascribe to Handel when he was in his forties. The last one, the sonata in D found in Book 6, is

---

430 Hutchings 89
431 Hutchings 23

from a later period and seems more reflective in tone. All three of the sonatas found in the Suzuki books were lumped together in the late nineteenth century by Chrysander into the collection titled Opus number 1. The origin of this early opus number was from an advertisement by Walsh in 1734 and has nothing to do with Handel's age when they were written.[432] Handel himself seemed to have had very little to do with the publication of these works.[433]

For more biographical information on George Frideric Handel see page 19. Information on his sonatas is on page 73.

JOHANN SEBASTIAN BACH
21 March 1685 – 28 July 1750
Concerto for Violin and Orchestra in A minor (BWV 1041)
Era: Baroque, written approximately 1730[434]
Genre: Baroque Dance Suite

Like the Double Concerto, the Concerto in A minor was either written for the court in Cöthen or the Collegium Musicum in Leipzig. If indeed Bach wrote it in Cöthen, it is possible that he wrote it for J.G. Pisendel (the man who was so keen to humiliate Veracini), J.B. Volumier or Joseph Spiess.[435] Bach was greatly influenced by Vivaldi's concertos, which at the time were popular throughout Europe. As a young man Bach had transcribed many of Vivaldi's violin concertos for the keyboard,[436] and it is difficult to believe that he hadn't used them as an inspiration for his own violin concertos:

> Bach was especially influenced by Vivaldi's coherent, well-defined ritornello[437] plans, his striking themes featuring short motifs ideally suited to soloistic elaboration, and his use of long

---

432 Loft 99

433 Loft 99

434 Wolff 357

435 Boyd 493

436 Boyd 493

437 Ritornello: A passage written for the full complement of instruments (and sometimes voices) that recurs in various guises during the course of a movement. Boyd 420.

cantilenas[438] underpinned by repeated bass ostinato[439] figures in the slow movements.[440]

Throughout Bach's concertos the orchestra plays an integral role, containing variation and organization that is interesting in its own right while allowing the soloist independence.[441] The opening movement of the Concerto in A minor has an extensive development of the opening ritornello, and the finale is a driving gigue with a ritornello form.[442] For more information on Bach see page 11.

JOHANN SEBASTIAN BACH
21 March 1685 – 28 July 1750
Gigue and Courante
Era: Baroque, written around 1720
Genre: Baroque Dance Suite

The unaccompanied Sonatas and Partitas for violin and for violin-cello are another instance of Bach taking hints from the past and basing structures of the utmost complexity upon them. . . By the end of the 17th century, the technique of polyphonic playing on a stringed instrument had been fully developed, particularly on the violin and the viol. But none of these men had written unaccom-panied music for a stringed instrument on any such scale as even one of the Bach works, let alone such a series of them as his two sets of six each.[443]

Gigue and Courante: from the Suite for Violoncello No. 1 in G Major, BWV 1007

---

438 The Harvard Dictionary of Music defines a cantilena as "a lyrical vocal melody or an instrumental melody of similar character." 144
439 The Harvard Dictionary of Music defines a bass ostinato as "a repeating melodic phrase set in the bass. . . and is usually from one to eight measures in length." 624.
440 Boyd 493
441 Boyd 493
442 Boyd 493
443 David 31

Gigue, like Bourrée in Book 3, is movement transposed from Bach's Cello Suites. Carl Bernhard Lienicke, principle cellist at Cöthen, could have been the man for whom these pieces were written. Christian Ferdinand Abel played viola da gamba, and could also have been the intended soloist. This Gigue and the following Courante are both from the first suite. The Gigue was traditionally the whirlwind end of the dance suite. "Gigue" probably comes from the word "jig," though it could have come from "giguer" ("to dance" in medieval French) or "Geige" ("violin" in German). Its origins are probably English:

In the 17th century British comedians popularized the jig on the European continent, and the association between these comedians and the dance form may have led to the use of the term jig with the meaning of joke, play, or game. In turn this led to the expression "the jig is up," meaning "the joke is over."[444]

Use of the word gigue would indicate that it is the French form of the dance, as opposed to the Italian "giga." French gigues are more complex, featuring a compound duple meter, rhythmic variety and, at times, counterpoint.[445] The Italian giga is "simpler, faster and more homophonic."[446] Allen Winold indicates that Gigue may be a combination of French and Italian styles.

The word "courante" is derived from the French verb for "running." As was the case for most elements of the Baroque dance suite, courantes were either written in the Italian or the French style. French courantes were more complex and refined than their Italian counterparts. An Italian corrente is robust and straightforward.[447] This courante, from the first cello suite, seems to be written in the Italian style. In the first part the tonal center wends from the tonic to the dominant. After the repeat it starts at the tonic, goes to the parallel minor and around to various tonal regions to finally end back at the tonic.[448]

For more biographical information on Johann Sebastian Bach see page 11.

---

444 Winold 77

445 Winold 77

446 Winold 77

447 Winold 45

448 Winold 45

ARCHANGELO CORELLI
17 February 1653 – 8 January 1713
Allegro
Era: Baroque, first published 1700
Genre: sonata for violin and keyboard

Allegro is a movement in Sonata no. 1 in D, one of Corelli's opus 5 chamber sonatas. (It was originally published in the same book as La Folia.) Abraham Loft suggests that, if possible, a combination of harpsichord and cello is a more authentic accompaniment than just a piano.[449] (During Corelli's day the harpsichordist would have improvised over a figured bass line.) Allegro is the third movement of this sonata. Loft writes that it is "a perpetual motion in sixteenths: the one violin line sketches out not only the conversation of two or more voices, but masses and textures of varying dimensions and density. And, under and almost around all this, the constantly striding bass line, outlining in its own leapings the functions of at least two simultaneously moving lines."[450]

Though it is possible for the more advanced student to ornament the fast movements of Corelli's sonatas (Geminiani, one of Corelli's own students, apparently did so), it is best for the performer to exercise restraint. See page 69 for biographical information and more detail on ornamentation in Corelli's Opus 5.

---

449 Loft 52
450 Loft 56

CHAPTER 8: SUZUKI BOOK 8

HENRY ECCLES
1675 (85?) – 1734 (45?)
Sonata in G Minor
Era: Baroque, Published 1720
Genre: Violin sonata

Little is known about Henry Eccles. As indicated above, even his birth and death dates are uncertain. He came from a family of musicians from England, and both he and his brother Thomas were violinists.[451] Henry was in the service of the Duke d'Aumont, ambassador from France, and lived in Paris when he published his two sets of violin sonatas (one in 1720 and one in 1723). Rumor, aided by Henry's alcoholic brother Thomas, indicated that Henry worked for the King of France. There is, however, no official record confirming this fact.[452]

The Sonata in G Minor has been transcribed for many instruments, most famously for the double bass. It is eleventh in the set published in 1720. Eccles dedicated the entire set to Sir William Gage, along with the statement that he had worked with all of his strength to compose it (*avec tous les soins possible!*).[453] Much of this set was, however, lifted directly from Giuseppe Valentini's *Allettamenti per camera* op. 8, so it is possible that the sonata in Suzuki Book 8 was not written by

---

451 Laurie 859
452 Laurie 859
453 Squire 790

Eccles.[454] The second set has an entirely different style from the first, which leads to speculation that these were taken from someone else.[455] A note on "borrowing" during the 18th century:

> It is generally accepted that the morality of composers in the 18th century was not sufficiently rigid to prevent them from borrowing ideas (and occasionally something more) from obscure predecessors or contemporaries. The remedy of a costly action for infringement of copyright did not exist, and it was only in exceptional cases . . . that public opinion, when such impudent thefts were exposed, chose to consider itself outraged.[456]

GRÉTRY, ANDRÉ ERNEST MODESTE
8 February 1741 – 24 September 1813
Tambourin
Genre: opera
Era: Classical, written 1794

André Ernest Modeste Grétry was a very successful composer of *opéras-comiques*. He lived in France before and after the Revolution and, like Gossec, managed to adapt himself successfully to each political situation as it came.

Grétry's father was a professional musician and violinist in Liège, France, where as a boy André was a member of the choir and also learned to play the violin.[457] Even more pivotal to his future, however, was the visit of Crosa Resta's Italian comic opera troupe from 1753-1755, when Grétry was a teenager.[458] Grétry's work as a young man was mostly in the area of symphonies and masses. At 19 Grétry moved to Rome, where he continued his musical education and at age 25 he went to Geneva, where he composed his first *opéra-comique* score.

---

454 Laurie 859
455 Squire 790
456 Squire 790
457 Charlton 385
458 Charlton 385

In 1767 Grétry made his final move, this time to Paris, where for two years he lived in obscurity and poverty.[459] Through a combination of good manners and charisma he eventually managed to secure the patronage of the Swedish Count of Creutz and the partnership of librettist Jean Francois Marmontel.[460] Marmontel and Grétry's first six operas made the composer quite popular and by 1769 he had become very wealthy and influential.[461] His speciality was *opera-comique*, a type of opera that was not "comedy" as we know it now but a genre in which song is interspersed with spoken dialogue.[462] Grétry's works were so well loved that between 1769 and 1824 the only month that went without one of his operas at the *Opéra-Comique* theater was February 1804.[463] As a family man Grétry was exemplary. He married and eventually had three daughters, as well as taking care of his mother and his deceased brother's children.[464]

Grétry wrote his own memoirs, in which he revealed (after the Revolution) that he had always been a secret republican, possibly to excuse his one-time employment as Queen Marie Antoinette's personal director of music.[465] He was particularly good at showing himself in the best possible light, a skill which probably explains his relatively long life despite starting out on the losing side of a bloody revolution. Though he survived the reign of terror unscathed and continued to write opera, Grétry never again enjoyed the heights of success that he had experienced before the Revolution. He was, however, given a job as instructor at the Beaux Artes along with Gossec and was named inspector of the Paris Conservatory of Music.[466] He resigned after one year and spent his remaining seventeen years in retirement.[467] During the reign of Napoleon Bonaparte he was given the Legion of Honor.[468]

---

459 Wickipedia "André Grétry"
460 Charlton 385
461 Charlton 385
462 Bartlet 477
463 Charleton, David. *Grétry and the Growth of Opera-Comique* 3
464 Charlton 385
465 Charlton 386
466 Warszawski http://www.musicologie.org/Biographies/g/gretry_andre.html
467 Cooper 44
468 Warszawski http://www.musicologie.org/Biographies/g/gretry_andre.html

When Grétry died the nation mourned, and several years and a furious lawsuit later his heart was buried in his hometown of Liège.[469]

In general his musical style combined Mannheim drive with Italianate melody.[470] Drama and music were inseparable to Grétry and "like Mozart, [he] strove to capture action in music and – as long as it was well motivated – was consistently inspired by a scene of activity."[471] Among his most famous works are *Zémir et Azor* (Beauty and the Beast) and *Richard the Lionheart.* Grétry's opera was popular all over Europe; Ludwig van Beethoven's father sang roles in two of his operas, and within and outside of France several of his operas were standards and well known throughout Europe.[472]

TAMBOURIN

Tambourin probably comes from one of Grétry's 69 operas. According to the Harvard Dictionary of Music, a "Tambourin" is a style based on a provincial French dance, used often in theatrical works during Grétry and Rameau's time. Its texture imitates a drum and pipe tune, probably familiar to the student of fiddle-type music of today. It has a "regular, static bass and a lively melody, usually in duple meter."[473]

G. Sabatini, who arranged Tambourin for woodwind quintet, suggests a metronome marking of 112 to the quarter note.

JOHANN SEBASTIAN BACH
21 March 1685 – 28 July 1750
Largo
Era: Baroque, written around 1720
Genre: Sonata for solo violin

---

469 Warszawski http://www.musicologie.org/Biographies/g/gretry_andre.html
470 Charlton 386. The Mannheim School, located in the German town Mannheim, specialized in exciting the audience with rhythmically and dynamically driven music. Italianate melody stems from the vocal parts of opera.
471 Charleton, David. *Gretry and the Growth of Opera-Comique* 10
472 Charleton, David. *Gretry and the Growth of Opera-Comique* 3
473 Randel 869

Bach never proceeded in a mechanical way; rather, he strove to give the arrangement an identity of its own by subjecting the model to further development and exhausting its potential. This often involved the addition of fresh contrapuntal parts, the alteration of detail and structural modification.[474]

J.S. Bach was influenced by many composers. Johann Pachebel was the teacher of his brother Johann Christian, the man who taught him how to play the organ. He was also inspired by his contemporaries Buxtehude, Reincken and Bohm.[475] Bach studied past masters, for example the works of the Renaissance composer Palestrina. In many ways he was, however, unique, with a style that was self-taught through private study and reflection.[476] Part of his appeal for contemporary musicians is the very complexity of his music. It is unique for its day, showing an intellectual as well as artistic approach that exploits all of the "possibilities of melody, harmony and counterpoint."[477]

Nothing shows Bach's complexity and beauty better than his *Sonatas and Partitas for Solo Violin*, a work written during his time in Cöthen and forgotten until long after his death. Like the Cello Suites, it is written as a set of six. The *Sonatas and Partitas* are now recognized as staples of violin repertoire that few other pieces can match. At the time it was not unheard of for composers to write for unaccompanied violin, but Bach was the first to write for the instrument in its full capacity.[478] Virtuoso violinists still consider a good performance of any of the unaccompanied sonatas and partitas to be a true display of skill.

LARGO

Largo comes from Sonata no. 3, in C Major, S 1005. The difference between a sonata and a partita is that a sonata was appropriate for church whereas a partita, as a series of dance movements, was not. ("Partita" is, in fact, another word for a dance suite).

---

474 Seaton343
475 Seaton 340e
476 Seaton 340
477 Winold 4
478 De Place

Like the cello suites, the sonatas and partitas were written the year Bach's first wife died. This Largo, though edited into a somewhat altered form for Suzuki Book 8, still has the same flowing lines and aria-like quality. One major difference between Bach's manuscript and the Suzuki book is that the manuscript is unaccompanied by keyboard – it accompanies itself by the chords that are played throughout. The original version contains double stops, which will be appropriate for the advanced student. (In the Suzuki books the accompanying line is taken by the piano.)

For more biographical information on Johann Sebastian Bach see page 11.

JOHANN SEBASTIAN BACH
21 March 1685 – 28 July 1750
Allegro
Era: Baroque, written after 1723
Genre: Continuo Sonata

This Allegro is from J.S. Bach's Sonata for Violin and Continuo, BWV 1023. It was written sometime after 1723. He and his family moved to Leipzig in May of 1723, so Allegro may have been written around the same time.

The move to Leipzig was both good and bad for Bach. The transition from Kapelmeister (music director of a court) to cantor was something of a step backward for him socially, and he was not the top choice of his new employers. As Seaton writes:

To [Bach], the Kantorate was a step downwards in the social scale, and he had little respect for his employers. To the council, Bach was a third-rater, a mediocrity, who would not do what they expected a Kantor to do – teach Latin, as well as organize the city church music. The stage was set for trouble, and in due course trouble came. [479]

The trouble with hiring a cantor for Leipzig was the duty of teaching Latin, which was the sticking point for most of the candidates. Georg Philipp Telemann, who was first choice for the job, refused to do it, as did the second one. (Telemann was so desirable to the city

---

479 Seaton 319

council that they hired him anyway, but he ended up staying with his old employers, who offered him more money.) Bach offered to pay another person to teach Latin, cinching the job for himself. It is hard to imagine that anyone would have expected one person to do all of the duties of music director as well as teach Latin, but it seemed that that was the case. Of course in hindsight we can all agree that J.S. Bach would have been a fantastic hire as music director for any school, but at the time he was merely a cantankerous fellow who had a reputation for writing music that was too difficult for his musicians to play (and then getting peeved with them).

On the other hand, in Leipzig Bach had a more stable financial base than he had had previously. He also had the benefits of a city with the foremost university in the German-speaking world just as his sons were reaching adulthood.[480] Living in a democratic system, rather than the court of an absolute prince, must also have been appealing. The duties of Kantor were much more varied and demanding than in the court of Cöthen, a fact which must have appealed to a man who enjoyed a challenge.[481]

For more biographical information on Johann Sebastian Bach see page 11.

PUGNANI, GAETANO
27 November 1731 – 15 July 1798
Largo Espressivo
Era: Classical, published before 1774
Genre: Continuo Sonata for Violin

Gaetano Pugnani, violinist and composer, was born and died in Turin Italy.[482] At age ten he secured a position as a second violinist in the orchestra at the Teatro Regio, a job which he kept until leaving Turin to study in Rome from 1749-50.[483] Between 1767 and 1769 he worked in London, where he published his first opera with great

---

480 Seaton 319
481 Seaton 319
482 Schwarz 589
483 Schwarz 589

success.[484] While there he also worked with Johann Christian Bach, J.S. Bach's youngest son.[485] By the time he turned 32 he had achieved the status of principal second violinist in the same orchestra he had played in as a child and had acquired an international reputation as a virtuoso.[486] By the end of his life Pugnani had taken over the position of first violinist of the King's Music, which included leadership of the Teatro Regio and other important positions in the musical life of Turin.[487]

Pugnani played with a great deal of power and was known for his *arco magno* (grand bowing).[488] He was, in fact, greatly influential in the evolution of the bow, helping to turn it into the instrument that we use today. Because he was interested in powerful sound he used a bow which was "straighter, longer, and equipped with a screw, and he may have exchanged views with the Parisian bowmaker Tourte pere in 1754 and with the younger François Tourte in 1772-3, both of whom were engaged in bringing the bow into its present form."[489] (Before Tourte standardized the bow that we know today, bows had no screws and were shorter. These early bows were capable of much less sound and fewer dynamic contrasts.)

Pugnani published his first composition in 1754 at age 23. He was excellent at orchestration and went on to compose pieces in most of the genres of his day. Pugnani was also notable as the teacher of the violinist Giovanni Battista Viotti, a man who would himself become a famous teacher.[490] Part of Pugnani's importance as a composer and pedagogue lies in his position as a bridge between two schools of violin technique: he himself was a student of G.B. Somis, who was a student of Corelli. It is thus through Pugnani that Viotti passed on the Corellian school to future generations of violinists.[491]

---

484 Schwarz 590

485 Adas *The Eighteenth Century Continuo Sonata, Volume VI.* xx

486 Schwarz 590

487 Adas *The Eighteenth Century Continuo Sonata, Volume VI.* xx

488 Schwarz 590

489 Schwarz 590

490 Schwarz 590

491 Adas *The Eighteenth Century Continuo Sonata, Volume VI.* xx

LARGO ESPRESSIVO

Largo Espressivo comes from Pugnani's Sonata No. 3 in D Major, Opus 8. It is one of the publication "Six SOLOS for a Violin and Bass, Most Humbly Dedicated to LORD COLERAINE by Gaetano Pugnani."[492] The notes are the same as the ones written in the original with the exception of the cadenzas (in measures 10-12 and last two measures), which were later additions. In Pugnani's day violinists would have made up their own cadenzas.

Largo Espressivo is the first movement of the sonata, and in the Urtext is merely labeled "Largo." The word "Espressivo" was probably added by a more Romantic editor, if we use the term "Romantic" to refer to more dramatic dynamics and emotion. The Opus 8 sonatas are all solo continuo sonatas, which are in form pre-Classical (even though these particular pieces fit within the Classical time period). Jane Adas explains that:

> For instrumental music, solo continuo sonatas represent in its purest form the polarity of outer parts so characteristic of Baroque music. They require only two lines of composed music – the upper melodic line for the soloist and the figured bass line for the continuo. . . The modern scholarly concept of a single musical ideal residing in the score is alien to the period.[493]

Adas is also adamant that an authentic rendition of this type of piece in Baroque style is just as challenging, and more accurate, than an attempt to romanticize it.[494] It seems likely, however, that Pugnani's *arco magno* would have made his own performances tend toward the greater dynamic contrasts of a Romantic interpretation. Historic precedence could go to either camp.

---

492 Adas *The Eighteenth Century Continuo Sonata, Volume VI.* 173
493 Adas *The Eighteenth Century Continuo Sonata, Volume VI.* x
494 Adas *The Eighteenth Century Continuo Sonata, Volume VI.* ix

FRANCESCO MARIA VERACINI
1 February 1690 – 31 October 1768
Sonata
Era: Baroque, published 1744
Genre: Baroque sonata

Sonata is no. 8 of Veracini's *Sonata accademica fuer Violine und Klavier Opus 2*, the same collection of twelve sonatas as Gigue from Sonata in D Major in Book 5. (Gigue comes directly before Sonata in the original manuscript.) Originally the Allegro con fuoco was the first movement, the Ritornello the second movement and the Giga the third movement. The other two movements, the Gavotte and Minuet contained in Suzuki Book 8, are not in the manuscript of Sonata no. 8 at all.[495] They appear later on, in Sonata no. 11 of Opus 2. For more information on Veracini and his Opus 2, see the entry for Gigue from Sonata in D Major on page 64.

---

495 Adas *The Eighteenth Century Continuo Sonata, Volume II*. 43

CHAPTER 9: BOOKS 9 AND 10

WOLFGANG AMADEUS MOZART
27 January 1756 – 5 December 1791
Concerto No. 5 in A Major, K. 219 (Book 9)
October 1775
Concerto in D Major, K. 218 (Book 10)
20 December 1775
Genre: Classical violin concerto

Wolfgang Amadeus Mozart wrote these two violin concertos in Salzburg at age 19, after his years as child prodigy and before his permanent move to Vienna. Three years prior he had joined his father Leopold at the court of the archbishop as the Konzertmeister, a paid position. His entire family was dissatisfied with the new archbishop, Hieronymus Colloredo. Colloredo both cut down the number and length of official musical performances and showed a preference for Italian musicians, neither of which boded well for the Mozart family.[496]

By 1775 Wolfgang was so disillusioned with his employer that he was writing the bare minimum of church music to scrape by at his job. He spent far more time writing instrumental music, encouraged to do so both by his father and, often, by the private patrons who paid him to do so.[497] In nine months' time he wrote four of his five

---

496 Eisen 281
497 Eisen 282

violin concertos, all in 1775, probably for Salzburg musicians such as Antonio Brunetti and not for himself.[498]

These two violin concertos show evidence of his growing maturity as a composer. Cliff Eisen's entry in the *New Grove Dictionary* indicates that both have affects, virtuosity and elements of surprise that had not been seen in Mozart's earlier works. Specifically in the A-Major Concerto "the soloist is introduced in the first movement by a poetic Adagio episode, and there is a notable 'Turkish' episode in the minuet finale."[499] The Turkish music, in fact, comes directly from Mozart's *Lucio Silla, le gelosie del Serraglio*, ballet music he had composed in 1772.[500] One interesting anecdote: Brunetti didn't like the soloist's opening notes, calling them "artificial." He requested something different, which Mozart obligingly wrote and can now be found as Adagio K261.[501] The D-Major Concerto's claim to innovation is in its finale, which was set "in a variety of tempos and meters."[502] This finale was very popular with the audience of its day because it was similar to the "Strasbourg," a fashionable dance.[503]

Mozart wrote these concertos at a time when violin music was used for all sorts of occasions, for example outdoor celebrations and intermezzo music at theaters.[504] Though Mozart played the violin very well and was at times admonished by his father to do more with the instrument, his twenty-seven piano concertos indicates a greater interest in the keyboard.[505] Mozart's influences seem to be Italian, in particular the *style galant* of Nardini and Pugnani (see Chapter 8). Above all the musician learning Mozart violin concertos should study his opera and incorporate a singing quality to the bow strokes.

---

498 Huggett jacket notes
499 Eisen 298
500 Dobretsberger jacket notes
501 Huggett jacket notes
502 Eisen 298
503 Dobretsberger jacket notes
504 Dobretsberger jacket notes
505 Dobretsberger jacket notes

AUTHOR'S NOTE
AND ACKNOWLEDGEMENTS

I began to be interested in the subject of the history of the Suzuki literature when I read Alex Ross's *The Rest Is Noise: Listening to the Twentieth Century*. The chapter that started it all was "Invisible Men," a history of early 20th century American composers. In particular I was struck by the fact that Antonin Dvořàk, who lived in the United States briefly, was very much influenced by the African-American students that he taught in the National Conservatory. Dvořàk himself came from the Czech peasant class and had become famous for incorporating folk tunes into his compositions.[506] When he lived in the United States his continued interest in the true "music of the people" led him to discover the uniqueness of his black students and to promote their work. Dvořàk felt very strongly that African-American music should be recognized, stating in a newspaper article that:

> I am now satisfied that the future music of this country must be founded upon what are called the [African] melodies. This must be the real foundation of any serious and original school of composition to be developed in the United States.[507]

Due to the racial climate of the times, most African-American composers and their contributions to classical literature eventually sank into obscurity. One of these students, Maurice Arnold Strothotte,

---

506 Ross 121
507 Ross 121

wrote *American Plantation Dances*, a section of which Dvořàk probably borrowed in his Humoresque.[508]

I felt like a door had been opened to me that I didn't know existed: so that was the inspiration for Humoresque! When I had the opportunity to write a paper for an independent history course I decided that what I really wanted to do was to find out more about the history of the pieces in the Suzuki literature. I was certain that there must be other fascinating stories out there, stories that my students needed to know.

Some of my discoveries have been surprising, for example, how many pieces in the repertoire were not written by the men to whom they were attributed. My suspicion about interesting anecdotes turned out to be true: Veracini once jumped out of a third story window in a fit of pique, J.S. Bach couldn't keep a job and Paganini came close to being buried alive as a child. Some of the stories are almost not fit for children to read. And, thus, this book was born!

I would like to acknowledge Robert Bussard and the staff at the Western Washington University Library, who helped me one summer as I dug through their materials. Janet Anderson and Jeff Simmons, friends who happen to be very well informed about just about everything, helped edit the paper and set me straight in my facts. Ben Gould edited my entire book for nothing but a few cups of coffee. It is through the websites of Kerstin Wartberg, head of the German Suzuki institute, that I discovered several of the BWV numbers for Bach's works. Thank you to Dr. Ed Rutschman the professor who advised me while writing the original paper (and let me do it for credit in the first place!).

There have been so many teachers who have helped me out through the years it is difficult to name them all! My music instructors set me on the path to my career as a violin teacher: thank you to Brenda Ramirez, Tim Brown, Andrea Een, Margaret Pressley, Grant Donnellan, Glen Spring and Steven Amundson. The Classics professors at St. Olaf College taught me to write a correct sentence. Any errors in grammar in this book are not their fault! (They convinced me that anyone who wants to write well should learn Latin.) Thank you to Richard DuRocher and Karen Cherewatuk, English teachers who had to deal with me on a regular basis at St. Olaf College. Rich sat me

---

508 Ross 124

down one day to tell me that if I wanted to write well I needed to find something of substance to write about. I've been trying to find that something ever since, and this is the result!

Finally, I would like to thank Kathleen Spring. She was my first violin teacher, became my mentor as I started my own studio and will be a lifelong friend. She encouraged me to continue writing after the original assignment was finished and turn it into a real reference book for Suzuki teachers and parents. Without her, this book would not have been written!

Appendix: Music History Games for your Students!

Baroque, Baroque, Classical

How to play: Essentially, this game is "duck, duck, goose," only using words that you would like your students to learn. First explain that "Baroque" means a certain era of music, as does "Classical." Perhaps give them an idea of the years involved, though the purpose of the game will just be to get them used to the words.

The students sit around in a circle (instruments go to the side with their parents). One child is chosen to stand up and walk around the circle, patting the heads of the other students and saying "Baroque, Baroque, Baroque…" until she finally touches one of the kids' heads and says "Classical!" She then has to run around the circle and land in the "Classical" kid's seat before he touches her. If she gets there first, then the child who was tagged has to go around and do the same thing.

Variants on this game: Ask the students to brainstorm composers of the Baroque or Classical era. Then they do, for example, "Bach, Bach, Mozart" or "Vivaldi, Vivaldi, Gossec." Also available are composers of the Romantic or Modern eras!

History Charades

Have groups of students choose an episode in music history, for example Lully stabbing himself with his baton. They then have to act it out in front of other students and let them guess who it is.

This game assumes a basic knowledge of music history.

Historical ABCs

Using a worksheet or a chalkboard, have the children write out the alphabet. Then they have to put down any composer that they can think of whose last name (or first, if you feel adventurous) begins with that letter.

Optional competitive game: separate into two teams and see which team gets the most names.

TIMELINE

Materials: a long roll of wrapping or butcher paper, markers, this book, other reference books, laptops, etc.

How to play: Roll out the paper. The teacher should write out the years between 1590 and the present in increments of 10 years prior to starting. Students must use the reference materials to fill out the timeline with the composers of the Suzuki books.

VARIANTS:

1) Speed timeline (especially appropriate for older kids). The students only have an hour to fill out the timeline.

2) Competitive/speed timeline (also appropriate for older kids). Two groups of students compete to fill out the timeline in an hour.

3) Eco-friendly timeline: use a chalkboard or white board to make the timeline.

4) Weekly timeline: Each week the students fill in whatever they can of the white board in the first ten minutes of group lesson. Take a picture of the timeline as the year goes on, showing them how much they have improved at the end of the year.

5) Homework timeline: Students each have a composer that they have to find a picture of to put in the timeline between group lessons. They could also be required to put in a fun fact about the composer, something that no one else knows about.

6) Long-term timeline: Take out the same roll of paper each week. Students continue to add to the same timeline throughout the year.

TRIVIA GAME

Materials: six sided die, index cards, die with as many sides as possible (100 sides is best), metronome, one minute timer.

Make up six categories. Before starting the game prepare the index cards. One category is music history. Prepare 20 music history questions for category 1. Category 2 is rhythms: write rhythms on index cards. Recognizing individual notes is category 3, and category 4 is recognizing Suzuki pieces that have been written down. Categories five and six can be a number of things: note reading, writing individual notes or the first four to six notes of Suzuki tunes. The hundred sided die is another optional category: the student has to roll the die to see how many hooked bows he or she can do in one up-bow.

The Game: Separate kids into two groups. Each rolls the six sided die to determine the category they have to answer. Use the one minute timer so that the game doesn't last forever. The first team to get ten points wins.

RANDOM FACTS GAME

Materials: white board or chalk board, pens or chalk.

Divide the group into two teams. Each one has access to this book and must pick a piece for the other team to play. While the team no. 1 is playing the piece, team no. 2 must write down every random fact about the composer and piece that they can come up with. Parents and laptops, iPhones and any other reference material may be used. Team no. 2 will then play while team no. 1 writes. The winning team is the team that writes down the most random facts about the piece.

TIMELINE

Note: only pieces that have specific dates are in the timeline.

1632 – November 29 Jean-Baptiste Lully born

1653 – February 17 Archangelo Corelli born

1675 – Henry Eccles born

1678 – March 4 Antonio Vivaldi born

1683 – September 25 Jean-Philippe Rameau born

1685 – February 23 George Frideric Handel born
March 21 Johann Sebastian Bach born

1686 – **Gavotte** (Lully/Marais)

1687 – March 22 Jean-Baptiste Lully died

1690 – February 1 Francesco Maria Veracini born

1700 – **La Folia, Allegro** (Corelli)

1703 – Jan 20 Joseph Hector Fiocco born

1706 – April 24 Padre Martini born

1707 – **Gavotte in G Minor** and **Minuet 1** (attributed to J.S. Bach)

1711 – **Bourée** (Handel)

       Concerto in A Minor (Vivaldi)

1712 – **Courante** (Corelli)

1713 – January 8 Archangelo Corelli died

1714 – **Musette** (Bach)

1717 – **Minuets 2 and 3** (attributed to J.S. Bach)

1720 – **Cello Suites: Bouree, Gavotte, Gigue** and **Courante** (J.S. Bach)

       Largo (J.S. Bach)

       Sonata in G Minor published (attributed to Eccles)

1723 – **Allegro** (J.S. Bach)

1724 – **Sonatas nos. 1 and 3** (Handel)

1729 – **Concerto in G Minor** (Vivaldi)

1731 – **Gavotte in D Major** (Bach)

       November 27 Gaetano Pugnani born

1734 – Jan. 17 François-Joseph Gossec born

       Henry Eccles died

1739 – November 2 Karl Ditters born

1741 – February 8 André Ernest Modeste Grétry born

June 21 Joseph Hector Fiocco died

July 28 Antonio Vivaldi died

1742 – **Gavotte** (Martini)

1743 – February 19 Luigi Boccherini born

1744 – **Sonata** and **Gigue from Sonata in D Minor** (Veracini)

1746 – **Chorus from *Judas Maccabeus*** (Handel)

1749 – **Sonata no. 4** (Handel)

1750 – July 28 Johann Sebastian Bach died

1756 – January 27 Wolfgang Amadeus Mozart born

1759 – April 14 George Frideric Handel died

1764 – September 12 Jean-Philippe Rameau died

1768 – October 31 Francesco Maria Veracini died

1770 – December 17 - Ludwig van Beethoven born

1771 – **Minuet** (Boccherini)

1774 – **Largo Espressivo** (Pugnani)

1782 – October 27 Nicolo Paganini born

1783 – **Minuet** (Mozart)

1784 – August 3 Padre Martini died

1786 - **Gavotte** (Gossec)
      November 18 Carl Maria von Weber born

1791 – December 5 Wolfgang Amadeus Mozart died

1795 – **Minuet in G** (Beethoven)

1798 – July 15 Gaetano Pugnani died

1799 – October 24 Karl Ditters von Dittersdorf died

1805 – May 28 Luigi Boccherini died

1810 - June 8 Robert Schumann born

1811 – August 5 Ambroise Thomas born

1813 – **Theme from *Witches' Dance*** (Paganini)
      September 24 André Ernest Modeste Grétry died

1817 – **"Hunter's Chorus"** (Carl Maria von Weber)

1826 – June 5 Carl Maria von Weber died

1827 – March 26 Beethoven died

1829 – Feb. 16 Francois-Joseph Gossec died

1833 – May 7 Johannes Brahms born
      May 11 Jean Becker born

1840 – **"The Two Grenadiers"** (Robert Schumann)
      May 27 Nicolo Paganini died

1841 – September 8 Antonin Dvorak born

1848 – **"Happy Farmer"** (Robert Schumann)
      June 12 Fritz Seitz born

1856 - July 29 Robert Schumann died

1866 – **Gavotte from *Mignon*** (Thomas)

1884 – Jean Becker died

1894 – **Humoresque** (Dvorak)

1896 – February 12 Ambroise Thomas died

1897 – April 3 Johannes Brahms died
1904 – May 1 Antonin Dvorak died
1912 – **Concerto no. 2** (Seitz)
1918 – May 22 Fritz Seitz died

PIECES CATEGORIZED BY COMPOSER:

Book numbers are indicated in parentheses.

Bach, Johann Sebastian: Allegro (8), Bouree (3), Concerto for Two Violins (4 and 5), Concerto No. 1 (7), Courante (7), Gavotte (5), Gavotte in D Major (3), Gavotte in G Minor (3), Gigue (7), Largo (8), Minuets 1, 2 and 3 (1 and 3), Musette (2)

Bayly, Thomas Haynes: *Long, Long Ago* (1 and 2)

Becker, Jean: Gavotte (3)

Beethoven, Ludwig van: Minuet in G (2)

Boccherini, Luigi: Minuet (2)

Brahms, Johannes: Lullaby (4), Waltz (2)

Corelli, Archangelo: Allegro (7), Courante (7), La Folia (6)

Dittersdorf, Karl Ditters von: German Dance (5)

Dvořàk, Antonín : Humoresque (3)

Eccles, Henry: Sonata in G Minor (8)

Gossec, François-Joseph: Gavotte (1)

Grétry, André Ernest Modeste.: Tambourin (8)

Fiocco, Joseph Hector: Allegro (6)

Handel, Georg Friedrich: Bouree (2), Chorus from *Judas Maccabeus* (2), Sonata No. 1 (7), Sonata No.3 (6), Sonata No. 4 (6)

Lully, Jean-Baptiste: Gavotte (2)

Martíni, (Padre) Giovanni Battista: Gavotte (3)

Mozart, Wolfgang Amadeus: Concerto in A Major (9), Concerto in D Major (10), Minuet (7)

Paganini, Niccolo: Theme from *Witches' Dance* (2)

Pezold, Christian: Minuets 2 and 3 (1 and 3)

Pugnani, Gaetano: Largo Espressivo (8)

Rameau, Jean-Philippe: Gavotte (6)

Schumann, Robert: "Happy Farmer" (1), "The Two Grenadiers" (2)

Seitz, Fritz: Concerto No. 2, 3rd Mvmt (4), Concerto No. 5, 1st and 3rd Mvmts (4)

Thomas, Ambroise: Gavotte from *Mignon* (2)

Veracini, Francesco Maria: Gigue from Sonata in D Minor (5), Sonata (8)

Vivaldi, Antonio: Concerto in A Minor (4 and 5), Concerto in G Minor (5)

Weber, Carl Maria von: Country Dance (5), Hunter's Chorus (2)

PIECES CATEGORIZED
BY TYPE OF COMPOSITION

Note: Many of these pieces fit into several categories. The bourrées, for example, are types of dances but also movements of sonatas.

Bourrée:
Bach (3), Handel (2)

Concerto
Bach, J.S.: Concerto for Two Violins in D Minor, Vivace; Concerto No. 1 (7)
Mozart: Concerto in A Major (10), Concerto in D Major (9)
Seitz: Concerto No. 2, 3rd Mvmt, Concerto No. 5, 1st Mvmt, Concerto No 5, 3rd Mvmt; Vivaldi: Concerto in A Minor, 1st and 3rd Mvmts (4) and 2nd Mvmt (5); Concerto in G Minor (5)

Courante
Bach (7); Corelli (7)

Folk Songs
Lightly Row, Song of the Wind, Go Tell Aunt Rhody, O Come Little Children, May Song

Gavotte
J.S. Bach (5), Bach, J.S. in G Minor (3), Bach J.S. (3), Becker (3), Gossec (1), Lully (2), Martini (3); Rameau (6), Thomas (2)

Gigue
J.S. Bach (7), Veracini (5)

Lullaby
Brahms (4), Schubert (4)

Humoresque
Dvorak (3)

Minuet
Bach, Minuets 1,2 and 3 (1) (Pezold), Minuet (3); Beethoven (2); Boccherini (2); Mozart (7)

Musette
Bach (2)

Opera
Handel: Chorus from *Judas Maccabeus* (2); von Weber: Hunter's Chorus (2), Gossec: Gavotte (1); Gretry, Tambourin; Thomas: Gavotte from *Mignon* (2)

Others
Schumann: Happy Farmer; Brahms: Waltz; Paganini: Theme from *Witches' Dance*; von Weber: Country Dance; Dittersdorf: German Dance; Fiocco: Allegro

Sonata
Bach: Largo (8), Allegro (8); Corelli, La Folia (6), Allegro (7); Eccles (8), Handel (7), Sonata No. 3 (6), Sonata No. 4 (6); Pugnani, Largo Espressivo (8); Veracini: Sonata (8)

Songs
Bayly *Long, Long Ago* (1 and 2); Schumann, "The Two Grenadiers" (2)

BIBLIOGRAPHY:

Adas, Jane, ed. *The Eighteenth Century Continuo Sonata, Volume II.* Garland Publishing, Inc; New York and London: 1991.

_____. *The Eighteenth Century Continuo Sonata, Volume VI.* Garland Publishing, Inc; New York and London: 1991.

Agay, Denes. Best Loved Songs of the American People. Doubleday and Company, Inc., Garden City New York: 1975.

Bach, J.S. *Klavierbuechlein fuer Anna Magdalena Bach 1725.* Ed. Georg von Dadelsen. Baerenreiter Kassel, Basel: 1957.

_____. *Kavierbuechlein fuer Wilhelm Friedemann Bach.* Ed. Wolfgang Plath. Baerenreiter Kassel, Basel: 1962.

_____. *Sechs Suiten fuer Violoncello Solo BWV 1007-1012.* Ed. Hans Eppstein. Baerenreiter Kassel, Basel: 1988.

_____. *The Three Violin Concerti in Full Score,* from the Bach-Gesellschaft edition. Dover Publications, New York: 1986.

Bachmann, Alberto. *An Encyclopedia of the Violin.* Da Capo Press, New York: 1966.

Baratz, Lewis Reece. " Joseph Hector Fiocco." *The New Grove Dictionary of Music And Musicians,* 2nd ed.

Edited by Stanely Sadie, MacMillan Publishers Limited, London: 2001.

Bartlet, M. Elizabeth C. "Opera Comique." *The New Grove Dictionary of Music And Musicians,* 2nd ed.

Edited by Stanely Sadie, MacMillan Publishers Limited, London: 2001. 477-484.

Bauer, Harold, ed. "Preface" to *Robert Schumann's Album for the Young op. 68.* G. Schirmer, Inc., New York: 1946.

Bergenfeld, Nathan. "Solving the Baroque Mysteries of Slides, Mordents and Trills." Clavier. Volume 42, No. 10. December 2003. 15-25.

Best, Terence. *Preface to George Friedrich Haendel: Sechs Sonaten fuer Violine und Basso Continuo*, herausgegeben von Johann Philipp Hinnenthal. Neueausgabe von Terence Best. Baerenreiter, Kassel: 2001.

Bohlin, Folke. "Dvorak, Antonin (Leopold)." *New Grove Dictionary of Music and Musicians*, 2nd ed. Edited by Stanley Sadie, MacMillan Publishers Limited, London: 2001. 777-815.

Borofsky, Howard. "Martini" *The New Grove Dictionary of Music and Musicians*, 2nd ed. Edited by Stanely Sadie, Macmillan Publishers Limited, London: 2001.

Boyd, Malcolm ed. *Oxford Composer Companion: J.S. Bach*. Oxford University Press, New York: 1999.

Bozarth, George S. and Walter Frisch. "Brahms, Johannes." *The New Grove Dictionary of Music and Musicians*, 2nd ed. Edited by Stanely Sadie, Macmillan Publishers Limited, London: 2001. 180-227.

Brook, Barry S., David Campbell, Monica H. Cohn and Michael Fend. "Gossec, Francois-Joseph." *The New Grove Dictionary of Music and Musicians*, Vol. 10, 2nd ed. Ed. Stanley Sadie. 186-190.

Burkholder, J. Peter, Donald Jay Grout and Claude V. Palisca. *A History of Western Music*, 7th ed. W.W. Norton and Company, New York: 2006.

Charleton, David and M. Elizabeth C. Bartlet. "André Ernest Modeste Grétry." *New Grove Dictionary of Music and Musicians*, 2nd ed. Edited by Stanley Sadie, MacMillan Publishers Limited, London: 2001. 385-394.

_____. *Grétry and the Growth of Opera-Comique*. Cambridge University Press, Cambridge: 1986.

Cooper, Martin. *Opéra Comique*. Max Parrish & Co Limited, London: 1949.

David, Hans T. and Arthur Mendel, eds. *The Bach Reader: A Life of Johann Sebastian Bach in Letters and Documents*. W.W. Norton & Co., New York: 1945.

Dean, Winton. *The New Grove Handel*. Norton and Company, New York: 1983.

_____. *Handel's Dramataic Oratorios and Masques*. Oxford University Press, London: 1959.

De Place, Adelaide. Notes to *J.S. Bach's Sonatas an Partitas for Solo Violin and Cello Suites*. EMI

Records Lt./Virgin Classics. Christian Tetzlaff and Ralph Kirschbaum, performers. 1993.

Dolbrechtsberger, Barbara, "Wolfgang Amadeus Mozart: Violin Concertos 1-5 Haffner Serenade" jacket notes to *Pamela Frank plays Mozart* (Tonhalle Orchester Zurich / David Zinman), Arte Nova Classics 74321 72104 2 (2000).

Eisen, Cliff. "Wolfgang Amadeus Mozart." The New Grove Dictionary of Music and Musicians, 2nd ed, ed.

Stanley Sadie. MacMillan Publishers Limited, London: 2001.

Elie, Rudolph. Jacket cover for the record *Arthur Grumiaux Violinist, Gregory Tucker Pianist: Johann*

Sebastian Bach Chaconne, Wolfgang Amadeus Mozart Sonatas and J. H. Fiocco Allegro. Boston Records.

Ewen, David. *The Complete Book of Classical Music: Biographies and critical evaluations of both major and minor composers from 1300 to 1900, and detailed notes on over one thousand musical works.* Prentice-Hall, Inc. Englewood Cliffs, New Jersey: 1965.

Foures, Olivier. Jacket notes to *Vivaldi: Giuliano Carmignola with the Venice Baroque Orchestra.* Archiv Productions for Deutsche Grammophon: 2006.

Fuld, James J. *The Book of World-Famous Music: Classical, Popular and Folk*, 3rd ed. Dover Publications, Inc, New York: 1985.

Fuller, David. "Suite." *The New Grove Dictionary of Music and Musicians*, 2nd ed, ed. Stanley Sadie. MacMillan Publishers Limited, London: 2001.

Garretson, Robert L. *Choral Music: History, Style, And Performance Practice.* Prentice Hall, New Jersey: 1993.

Geck, Martin. *Johann Sebastian Bach: His Life, Work and Influence 1685-1750.* Inter Nations, Bonn: 2000.

George, David L, ed. *The Family Book of Best Loved Poems.* Doubleday and Company, Inc; Garden City, New York: 1952.

Gibbs, Christopher H. "Beyond song: instrumental transformations and adaptations of the Lied from Schubert to Mahler." *The Cambridge Companion to the Lied.* Edited by James Parsons. Cambridge University Press, Cambridge: 2004. 223-242.

Gorce, Jerome de la. "Jean-Baptiste Lully." *The New Grove Dictionary of Music and Musicians*, 2nd ed. MacMillan Publishers Limited, London: 2001. 292-308

Grave, Margaret. "Dittersdorf, Carl Ditters von." *The New Grove Dictionary of Music and Musicians*, 2nd ed. MacMillan Publishers Limited, London: 2001. 385-391.

Grout, Donald J. and Hermine Weigel Williams. *A Short History of Opera.* 3rd ed. Columbia University Press, New York: 1988.

Hale, Philip. Biographical sketch in Robert Schumann's *Album for the Young.* G. Schirmer, Inc., New York: 1945.

Heartz, Daniel. "Galant." *The New Grove Dictionary of Music and Musicians*, 2nd ed. Edited by Stanley Sadie. MacMillan Publishers Limited, London: 2001.

Heller, Karl. *Antonio Vivaldi: The Red Priest of Venice.* Amadeus Press, Portland, Oregon: 1991.

Heyer, John Hajdu, ed. "Introduction." *Jean-Baptiste Lully and the Music of the French Baroque: Essays in Honor of James R. Anthony.* Cambridge University Press, Cambridge: 1989.

Hicks, Anthony. "Handel, George Frideric." *The New Grove Dictionary of Music and Musicians, volume 10.* 2nd ed. Ed Stanley Sadie. MacMillan Publishers Limited, London: 2001. 747-813

Hsu, John, ed. *Marin Marais: The Instrumental Works Vol. 1: Pieces for One or Two Viols, 1686-89.* Broude Brothers Limited, New York: 1980.

Huggett, Monica. "Mozart: The Violin Concertos" jacket notes to Mozart: The 5 Violin Concertos (London / Huggett), CD 7243 5 61578 2 (1999).

Hutchings, A.J.B. *The Baroque Concerto.* W.W. Norton and Company, New York: 1961.

Jameson, Michael. Liner notes to *Concertos from my Childhood. Itzhak Perlman: Concertos from my Childhood: Rieding, Seitz, Accolay, Beriot, Viotti.* EMI Records Ltd, New York: 1999.

Joachim, J. and F. Chrysander. *Les Oevres de Archangelo Corelli revues par J. Joachim and F. Chrysander. Book V Op. 6 Part II.* Galliard Limited, London : (no date).

Kenyon, Nicholas. Liner notes to *Nicolo Paganini: Denes Zsigmondy, Violin.* CMS Records, Inc., New York: 1978. (Record: SUMMIT SUM 5049)

Kerman, Joseph. "Beethoven, Ludwig van." *The New Grove Dictionary of Music and Musicians*, 2nd ed.

Edited by Stanley Sadie. MacMillan Publishers, Limited, London: 2001. P. 73-140.

Kilian, Dietrich ed. *J.S. Bach: Konzerte fuer violine, fuer zwei violinen, fuer cembalo, floete und violine.* Baerenreiter Kassel, Basel: 1986.

Kneip, Gustav, ed. Deutschland im Volkslied: 714 Lieder aus den deutschprachigen Landschaften und aus Europa. C.F. Peters, London: 1958.

Kolneder, Walter. „Preface" to *Veracini Sonata Accademica Fuer Violine und Klavier, Opus II Nr. 8 in e moll.* Edition Peters, Leipzig: 1970.

Krull, Kathleen. *Gonna Sing my Head Off! American Folk Songs for Children.* Scholastic, New York: 1993.

Kuhn, Laura, ed. "Martini, Giovanni Battista." *Bakker's Biographical Dictionary of Musicians*, Vol. 4. Schirmer Books, New York: 2000.

Laurie, Margaret. "Henry Eccles (ii)." *The New Grove Dictionary of Music and Musicians*, 2ⁿᵈ ed. Edited by Stanley Sadie. MacMillan Publishers Limited, London: 2001. P. 859.

Lipscomb, Jeffrey J "... Leaves; Piano Pieces; Mazurkas; Moderato in A; "Question"; Impromptu in d; "Poetic Tone Pictures"; Humoresques; "Dumka"; "Furiant"; "Two Little Pearls"; "Album Leaf in E-flat"; Suite in A, "American"; hit Humoresque in F#; Lullaby; Capriccio" *Fanfare - The Magazine for Serious Record Collectors* 29:3 (January-February 2006). p. 101-102

Longyear, Rey M. *Nineteenth-Century Romanticism in Music.* Prentice Hall, Englewood Cliffs, New Jersey: 1988.

Lyons, James. Notes from the jacket of *David and Igor Oistrakh play the Bach Concerto for Two Violins and Orchestra.* Monitor Collectors series.

Mill, Albert. "Becker, Jean." *The New Grove Dictionary of Music and Musicians, 2ⁿᵈ ed.* Edited by Stanley Sadie. MacMillan Publishers Limited, London: 2001. P. 49.

Miyama, Yoshio. Liner notes for *Boccherini 4 String Quartets.* PCM Digital, Siemens Villa, Berlin: 1987.

Nippon Columbia CO, Ltd.

Nelson-Burns, Lesley. *Long, Long Ago.* http://www.contemplator.com/england/longago.html. Viewed May 8, 2009.

Neufeldt, Victoria, ed. *Webster's New World Dictionary of American English.* Prentice Hall, New York: 1994.

Pauly, Richard G. *Music in the Classic Period, 4ᵗʰ ed.* Prentice Hall, New Jersey: 2000.

Peress, Maurice. *Dvorak to Ellington: A Conductor Explores America's Music and its African American Roots.* Oxford University Press, New York: 2004.

Pinkert-Sältzer, Inke ed. *German Songs: Popular, Political, Folk and Religious.* Continuum, New York: 1997.

Pitou, Spire. *The Paris Opera: An Encyclopedia of Operas, Ballets, Composers, and Performers, Rococo and Romantic, 1715-1815.* Greenwood Press, London: 1985.

Randel, Don Michael ed. *The Harvard Bibliographical Dictionary of Music.* The Belknap Press of Harvard University Press, Cambridge, Massachusetts: 1996.

Rivers, Travis. "Friedrich (Fritz) Seitz."

Robison, Judith. Notes to the LP *Bach Goes to Town: Igor Kipnis Plays his Happiest Encores for Harpsichord.* Producer George Sponhaltz, Engineer Carson C. Taylor. Capitol Records, Inc: 1976.

Rosen, Charles. Sonata Forms. W.W. Norton & Company, New York: 1980.

Ross, Alex. *The Rest is Noise: Listening to the Twentieth Century*. Farrar, Straus and Giroux, New York: 2007.

Sadie, Stanley. "Mozart: Wolfgang Amadeus Mozart." *The New Grove Dictionary of Music and Musicians, volume 10*. 2nd ed. Ed Stanley Sadie. MacMillan Publishers Limited, London: 2001.276-347.

Schmitz, Hans-Peter. Forward to *George Friedrich Haendel: Elf Sonaten fuer Floete und Bezifferten Bass*. Baerenreiter Kassel, Basel: 1955.

Schumann, Robert. *Album for the Young, op. 68*. Edited according to manuscripts and her personal recollections by Clara Schumann. Belwin Mills Publishing Corp, Melville, N.Y.: (no date).

Schumann, Robert. *Vocal Album: Fifty-five Songs for Low Voice*. G. Schirmer, Inc., New York: 1930.

Schwartz, Boris and Maurita P. McClymonds. "Gaetano Pugnani." *The New Grove Dictionary of Music and Musicians, volume 10*. 2nd ed. Ed Stanley Sadie. MacMillan Publishers Limited, London: 2001. 589-591.

Scott, R.H.F. *Jean-Baptiste Lully*. Peter Owen, London: 1973.

Seaton, Douglas. "J.S. Bach." *New Grove Dictionary of Music and Musicians*. Etc.

Squire, W. Barclay. "Henry Eccles Borrowings." *The Musical Times*, Vol. 64, No. 969. (Nov. 1 1923), pp. 790.

Starr, William. Interview.

Straeten, E. van der. *The History of the Violin: its Ancestors and Collateral Instruments from Earliest Times to the Present Day*. Cassell and Company, Ltd., London: 1933.

Stratton, Stephen. *Nicolo Paganini: His Life and Work*. Greenwood Press; Westport, Conneticut: 1971.

Suzuki, Shinichi. *Nurtured by Love: The Classic Approach to Talent Education*. Sumy-Birchard,Inc.; Miami: 1983.

Talbot, Michael. "Vivaldi." *The New Grove Dictionary of Music and Musicians, 2nd ed*. Edited by Stanley Sadie. MacMillan Publishers Limited, London: 2001. 817-843.

Warrack, John. *Carl Maria von Weber*. 2nd ed. Cambridge University Press, Cambridge: 1976.

_____. Synopsis from CD cover of Carl Maria von Weber's *Der Freischutz*. Rundfunkchor Leipzig and Staatskapelle Dresden, directed by Carlos Kleiber. Deutsche Gramophon recording, 1998.

Warszawski, Jean-Marc. "Andre Gretry." http://www.musicologie.org/Biographies/g/gretry_andre.html.
Viewed January 19, 2009.

Wartberg, Kerstin. *Information for Violin Teachers about Antonio Vivaldi (1678-1741): Concerto in A Minor for Violin Solo and String Orchestra Op 3, No 6; RV 356.*

White, Chappell. *From Vivaldi to Viotti: A History of the Early Classical Violin Concerto.* Gordon and Breach, Philadelphia: 1992.

Winold, Allen. *Bach's Cello Suites: Analyses and Explorations. Volume 1: Text.* Indiana University Press, Bloomington and Indianapolis: 2007.

Wolff, Christoph. *Johann Sebastilan Bach: The Learned Musician.* W.W. Norton and Company, New York: 2000.

Wissick, Brent. "Lully Gavotte." *American Suzuki Journal.* Fall, 1996. 46-7.

CPSIA information can be obtained at www.ICGtesting.com
Printed in the USA
LVOW071949170113

316152LV00023B/1703/P